## KATRIN CARGILL

# simple
# soft furnishings

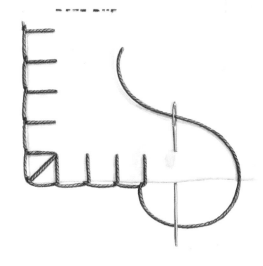

# KATRIN CARGILL

# simple
# soft furnishings

## 50 stylish sewing projects to transform your home

photography by David Montgomery

FIREFLY BOOKS

# A FIREFLY BOOK

Published by Firefly Books Ltd. 2004

First printing

Publisher Cataloging-in-Publication Data    (U.S.)
Cargill, Katrin.
    Simple soft furnishings : 50 stylish home sewing projects to transform your
home / Katrin Cargill ; photography by David Montgomery. –1st ed.
[192] p. : col. ill., photos. ;   cm.
Includes index.
Summary: Practical guide with illustrated step-by-step instructions to sewing
50 original soft furnishing design projects, including cushions, curtains, blinds,
seating, bedding and table linens.  Includes list of resources and suppliers.
ISBN 1-55407-018-X  (pbk.)
1.  Interior decoration.  2. Sewing.  I.  Montgomery, David.  II.  Title.
646.2  dc22   TT707.C37   2004

Library and Archives Canada Cataloguing in Publication
Cargill, Katrin
    Simple soft furnishings : 50 stylish sewing projects to transform your home
/ Katrin Cargill ; photography by David Montgomery.
Includes index.
ISBN 1-55407-018-X
    1.  Sewing. 2.  House furnishings. 3.  Interior decoration—Amateurs'
    manuals.  I.  Title.
    TT387.C37 2004    646.2'1    C2004-903601-7

Published in the United States in 2004 by
Firefly Books (U.S.) Inc.
P.O. Box 1338, Ellicott Station
Buffalo, New York 14205

Published in Canada in 2004 by
Firefly Books Ltd.
66 Leek Crescent
Richmond Hill, Ontario L4B 1H1

**Editorial Director**  Jane O'Shea
**Creative Director**  Helen Lewis
**Project Editor**  Lisa Pendreigh
**Designer**  Sue Storey
**Photographer**  David Montgomery
**Stylist**  Katrin Cargill
**Illustrator**  Carolyn Jenkins
**Production Director**  Vincent Smith
**Production Controller**  Rebecca Short

The publisher has endeavoured to ensure
that all project instructions are accurate.
However, due to variations in readers'
individual skills and materials available, the
publisher cannot accept responsibility for
damages or losses resulting from the
instructions herein. All instructions should
be studied and clearly understood before
beginning any project.

Printed in China

# contents

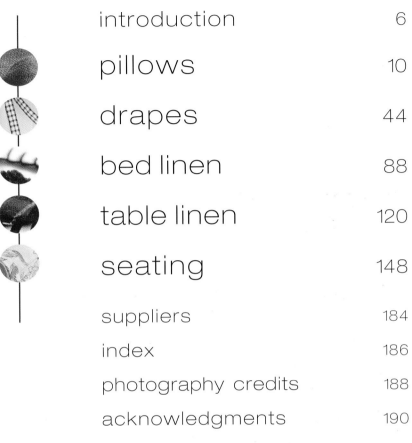

introduction                6

pillows                    10

drapes                     44

bed linen                  88

table linen               120

seating                   148

suppliers                 184

index                     186

photography credits       188

acknowledgments           190

# introduction

The busier our lives and the less secure the outside world becomes, the more we want to cocoon ourselves in our homes. And the more conscious we are of our home environment. As a result, the home furnishings industry—from furniture superstores to fancy fabric houses—has boomed over the last few decades. With the plethora of interiors books and magazines, it's hard not to want our houses to resemble the glossy images that bombard us. But creating the individual style we are most comfortable with, be it farmhouse country or city chic, doesn't comes easily to most of us. Either we try to put together a "look" ourselves, or we have to use an interior designer—at considerable expense. So, it is a good idea to gather as much information and knowledge as possible. Cut out photos from magazines to create a file of favorite looks, collect paint and fabric samples that you like and, before you know it, you will have honed down your personal style—something unique to you.

I grew up as a rather nomadic child, living everywhere from Tunisia to America, via Scandinavia and England, so my immediate home surroundings have always been very important to me. Getting nested in a new home meant fixing up my bedroom as a matter of urgency. Usually it took a coat of paint in one of the colors of the moment (during my teenage years it was a groovy luminous orange) and, if I was lucky, I got a new pair of curtains, a bedspread and some pillows. Gradually I developed a color palette of my own and, as I travel and see new color combinations and styles, so my look develops and changes.

The next step is to implement these ideas in your home. You can transform a room dramatically with a few new soft furnishings. Because the projects in this book are easy to make, you won't be stuck with them forever; when styles and colors change, so can your home with a few quick and easy sewing ideas.

*Simple Soft Furnishings* is divided into five sections: pillows, with everything from a basic bed bolster to a gathered round plump pillow; drapes and blinds, ranging from a simple no-sew drape to a more sophisticated contrast-lined roman blind; bed linens, filled with fun bedspread ideas; table linens, including cute gingham napkins

with velvet edging; and seating, which is filled with ideas from a simple loose cover to a fitted chair cover with box pleats. Each chapter is devoted to ideas that can take mere moments, like the Lace-edged Coverlet on page 90, or more personal projects that involve some planning and a bit of hand stitching, like the Crib Quilt with Embroidered Initial on page 110.

One of the first challenges is choosing your fabric. The projects in *Simple Soft Furnishings* call for fabrics made of natural fibers — cotton, linen, wool and silk. But fabric stores today are filled with a wealth of good-quality man-made fibers, fiber blends and fleeces that can make very beautiful and successful soft furnishings as well. And they may even be better suited to your budget. Many people are overwhelmed at first by the amazing selection. But if you go back to your basic file of favorite looks, you may find you have a relatively small range of fabrics, colors and textures that really attracts you. Stick with those. Remember, too, to be practical. A loose sofa cover made from a heavy unwashable cloth doesn't make sense; a dark, dye-laden fabric for bedding or a table project might cause problems later. If in doubt, prewash a sample to see how it reacts.

I have deliberately used strong colors to create graphic images, so you may want to adapt the colors to your own palette. Because so many of these projects are simple, attention to detail is paramount. Combining colors is important, and details like trimmings, beadings and ribbons go a long way toward creating a really great stylish product.

This book has been designed not only to inspire you to transform your home but also just to get you sewing. Many of the projects can be made by simple hand stitching, but of course a sewing machine will make the job much easier. It really does make sense to be as well equipped as possible — and a good sewing machine will be with you for life. A solid work surface for cutting fabric is also useful and good light is essential. Don't scrimp on scissors, pins, tape measure or cotton thread, as you will only compromise your efforts.

Happy sewing!

pillows

# simple pillow

This basic pillow uses a simple stitched overlap closure, so you don't need to wrestle with any tricky fastenings. The pillow form slips neatly into the opening at the back, making it convenient for laundering.

**Materials**

Fabric, such as lightweight cotton or linen

Sewing thread

Ready-made monogram or embroidery floss

Pillow form

1 For the front panel, cut a piece of fabric to the size of the pillow form, adding ¾" (2 cm) seam allowance all the way around. For the back panels, cut a piece of fabric the same length but half the width of the pillow form plus 1⅜" (3.5 cm), and adding ¾" (2 cm) seam allowance on the other three sides. Cut another piece of fabric half the width of the pillow form plus 4¾" (12 cm) to the width, and adding ¾" (2 cm) seam allowance on the other three sides.

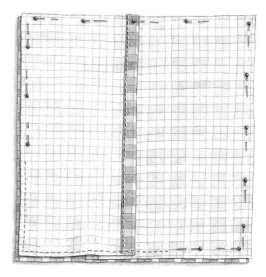

*step 3*

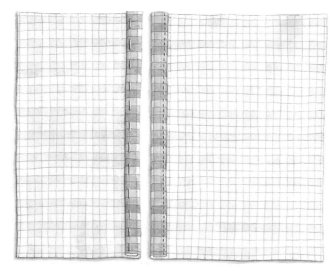

*step 2*

2 Lay the two back panels right sides down and turn in a double ⅜" (1 cm) hem on one short side of each. Pin, baste and then stitch. Press.

3 If using a ready-made monogram, apply it to the front panel. With right sides together, lay the two back panels over the front panel with raw sides edge to edge so that the two seamed edges overlap by 3½" (9 cm). Pin or baste together ⅜" (1 cm) from edges. Stitch. Turn right side out. Press. If required, hand sew a monogram using embroidery floss to the front of the pillow. Insert the pillow form.

## adding a monogram

Sometimes it is possible to find old ready-made monograms in antique sales
that can be hand sewn onto pillows. Old linens often yield monograms that can
be cut out as patches and appliquéd to the front of pillows, either by hand, using
embroidery floss and blanket stitch, or with a zigzag stitch on the machine.
Cut around the monogram with sharp scissors, turn under on all sides, press
and attach to the front of the pillow. It is best to do this before sewing the pillow
pieces together in step 2. Hand embroidering a monogram is also special; use
embroidery floss and work it in cross stitch or back stitch.

# trimmed pillow

Incorporating rickrack, fringing or welting into the edges of a pillow is always done with the same technique: sandwich and secure them between the front and back panels of the pillow.

## Materials

As for Simple Pillow (see page 12)

Rickrack, piping or other trim

Pillow form

## trimming a pillow with rickrack

Make the front and back panels as shown in steps 1 and 2 of the Simple Pillow (see page 12). If preferred, use different fabrics for the front and back panels. With the front panel right side up, lay the rickrack trimming around the edges of the fabric so that the middle of its width is ⅜" (1 cm) from the raw edges. Pin in place. Baste along the middle of the rickrack. With right sides together, lay the two back panels over the front panel with raw sides edge to edge so that the two seamed edges overlap, as shown in step 3 of the Simple Pillow (see page 12). Pin or baste together ⅜" (1 cm) from edges. Stitch very carefully along this line so it follows the middle of the rickrack. Turn right side out. Press. Insert the pillow form.

## trimming a pillow with welting

When using welting to trim a pillow, lay the welting around the edges of the front panel so the raw sides of the panel and the selvage of the welting are edge to edge and the cord side lies ⅜" (1 cm) inside the pillow edge. Lay the two back panels with right sides together over the front panel, with raw sides edge to edge so that the two seamed edges overlap, as shown in step 3 of the Simple Pillow (see page 12). Pin or baste together ⅜" (1 cm) from edges. Stitch carefully along this line so it is as close as possible to the cord. Turn right side out. Press. Insert the pillow form.

---

## incorporating trims

Trims without selvages, such as rope borders, velvet ribbons or beads, can also be used; these need either to be applied to the front panel after it has been cut out and before joining it with the back, or to be sewn on once the pillow has been stitched together.

# ruffle-edged pillow

One of the quickest and most effective ways of freshening up a tired-looking room is to add some new throw pillows. There is always a huge selection available in the stores, but when you realize how easy it is to make your own, you will be able to transform a room in a weekend. And what is a more refreshing fabric than simple cotton ticking?

# ruffle-edged pillow

## Materials

Fabric, such as cotton ticking

Sewing thread

Zipper that is 4" (10 cm) shorter than the width of the pillow form

Pillow form

Add a softly gathered ruffle to a plain pillow and the look is as comfortable in a country setting as in a minimalist interior. Easy-to-follow instructions for putting in a zipper are given here to add a useful sewing skill to your repertoire.

1 For the front panel, cut a piece of fabric to the size of the pillow form, adding ¾" (2 cm) seam allowance all the way around. For the back panels, cut two pieces of fabric the same length but half the width of the pillow form, adding ¾" (2 cm) seam allowance all the way around. For a 2½" (6.5 cm) deep ruffle, cut a strip of fabric 2½ times the perimeter of the pillow form by 6½" (16.5 cm). If necessary, join pieces together to achieve the required length.

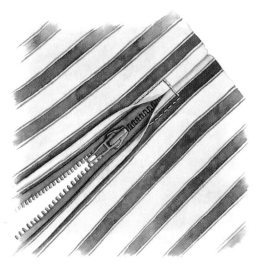

*step 3*

*step 2*

2 For the back panel, place the two back panels right sides together and stitch 2" (5 cm) in from each outside edge with a ¾" (2 cm) seam allowance. Open out the seams and press along both stitched and unstitched sections.

3 Turn the back panel right side up and lay the closed zipper right side up underneath the opening, between the two seams, ensuring that the fabric meets over the middle of the zipper. Pin and baste the zipper in place. Slip stitch the opening along the pressed edges so they meet. Top stitch down one side, across the end and up the other side of the zipper, using a zipper foot if machining. Remove the slip stitches. Open the zipper before you continue.

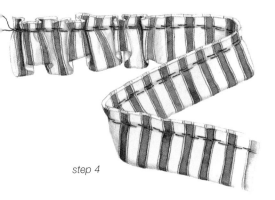

*step 4*

4 For the ruffle, stitch together the two short
ends, leaving a ¾" (2 cm) seam allowance to
make a continuous band. Open out the seam and
press. Fold the sewn band in half widthwise with the
right side out and press. Hand sew a double row of
running stitches ¾" (2 cm) from the open edge. Pull
the threads to form even gathers until the band is
the same size as the perimeter of the pillow form.

*step 5*

5 With the front panel right side up, lay the
gathered ruffle around the perimeter of the
front panel so that the raw edges are edge to edge.
Pin and baste the ruffle ¾" (2 cm) from the outside
edge. Place the back panel over the top, right side
down. Pin and baste together ¾" (2 cm) from edges.
Stitch carefully around all four sides just inside this
line so that the gathering stitches of the ruffle are not
visible. At each corner, work the stitches in a curve
rather than a right angle. Trim the edges and clip the
corners. Turn right side out through the zipper
opening. Press. Insert the pillow form.

# scallop-edged pillow

The elegant curves of a scalloped flange add sophistication to household cotton ticking, as they would to almost any other fabric. The corners of the scallops are mitered to form a flange for the pillow.

1 Make the front and back panels with a zipper opening as shown in steps 1, 2 and 3 of the Ruffle-edged Pillow (see page 18). For the scalloped edge, cut four strips of fabric to the width of the pillow form, adding 1" (2.5 cm) seam allowance, by 3" (7.5 cm) plus 1" (2.5 cm) seam allowance. Cut a further four strips of fabric to the length of the pillow form plus 1" (2.5 cm) seam allowance by 3" (7.5 cm) plus 1" (2.5 cm) seam allowance.

2 For the scalloped edge, lay one long strip right side up. Place a short strip on top, right side down, aligning with one corner. Fold then press the

corner at a 45-degree angle. Pin and baste along the fold. Stitch. Trim the excess fabric to a ⅜" (1 cm) seam allowance. Repeat this for the remaining three corners until you have a rectangular frame. Open out all the corner seams and press. Make a second

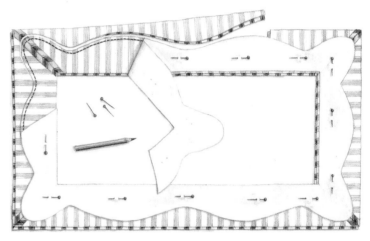

*step 3*

3 Lay the two frames together, right sides facing. Using a paper template, draw the outer edge of the scallop shapes onto the wrong side of the top frame. Remove template. Pin and baste. Stitch all around the outline. Trim the excess fabric to a ⅜" (1 cm) seam allowance and snip the curves. Turn right side out. Follow step 5 for Ruffle-edged Pillow to finish.

*step 2*

## Materials

Fabric, such as cotton ticking

Sewing thread

Zipper that is 4" (10 cm) shorter than the width of the pillow form

Paper template for scallop shape

Pillow form

# bolster with silk ties

Bolsters serve all sorts of practical and decorative purposes. Awkward angular gaps on sofas, bed ends and day beds can be visually minimized by a plump bolster. Introduce rich color, texture or pattern into a room with a bolster cover to add a chic accent.

# bolster with silk ties

The contrast of turquoise cotton toile de Jouy fabric and the gorgeous iridescent emerald green silk ties on this bolster make a strong, stylish statement. The simple bolster is quick and easy, and can be made from almost any fabric.

*steps 1 and 2*

**1** Cut a piece of fabric to the circumference of the bolster form, adding ¾" (2 cm) seam allowance by the length of the bolster plus twice the required overhang (approximately 16"/40.5 cm) here). If the fabric is too narrow, join extra pieces to either end. Fold in half the length of each overhang and press. Stitch ⅜" (1 cm) from the folded-in edge.

**2** Fold fabric in half lengthwise with right sides together. Pin and baste. Stitch ¾" (2 cm) from the edge. Open out seams and press.

**Materials**

Fabric, such as medium-weight cotton

Sewing thread

Fabric for making ties, such as silk

Bolster form

*step 3*

**3** To make the tie, cut a piece of silk 20" (51 cm) wide by 40" (101.5 cm) long and fold in half lengthwise. Press. Draw a line at a 45-degree angle on both ends and snip off the excess triangles of silk. Baste the long open side and one short end ⅜" (1 cm) from the raw edges, and stitch. Turn right side out and fold in the raw edges of the open end. Use small, neat slip stitches to close the opening. Press.

## alternative bolster ties

As an alternative to silk ties, use contrasting velvet ribbon and little gingham roses
for a more decorative effect. Scour flea markets or garage sales for old ribbon and
scraps of antique textiles to contrast with a modern fabric. To make the gingham
roses, follow the instructions for the rosette on page 29.

# gathered round pillow

Pretty and pert, round pillows add a touch of high fashion to any room. Sometimes a space calls for something just that little bit more special than the ubiquitous knife-edged pillow, and this one with circular pleats and a decorative rosette certainly looks unique.

# gathered round pillow

Unless you are a very experienced sewer, this pillow is easiest to make from a sturdy, tightly woven yet thin fabric so that the pleats won't slip away. The closure is buttoned, although you could opt for a zipper.

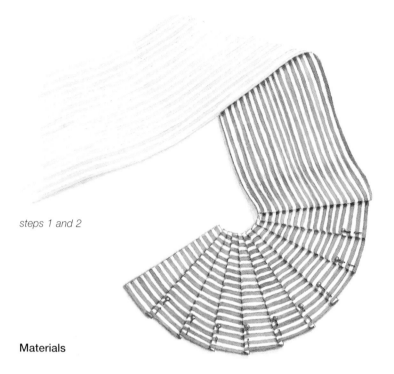

*steps 1 and 2*

### Materials

Fabric, such as a tightly woven, crisp cotton

Sewing thread

Circular pillow form

1 For the front panel, cut a length of fabric one and two-thirds times the circumference of the pillow form by the radius of the pillow form plus ¾" (2 cm) seam allowance all the way around. If necessary, join pieces of fabric together to achieve the required length.

2 Fold in and pin pleats around the circle so that around the outer edge they are approximately 2" (5 cm) wide with a tuck-under of one-third that width. Secure with basting stitches. Pin and baste

the two open ends together to hide the raw edges. Gather the pleats around the inner edge to close the center gap. Secure with basting stitches. Stitch the seam to close the raw edges. Stitch the outer circumference ¾" (2 cm) from the edge.

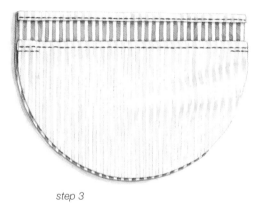

*step 3*

3 For the back panel, draw and cut a semicircle the diameter of the pillow form plus ¾" (2 cm) seam allowance plus 1½" (3.75 cm) on the straight side. Cut another semicircle with ¾" (2 cm) seam allowance plus 4" (10 cm) on the straight side. Turn under ½" (1.25 cm) on both straight sides. Press and stitch. With right sides up, line up the semicircles to form a circle and pin together. Stitch 2" (5 cm) in from both outside edges along the straight side of the shorter piece with a ¾" (2 cm) seam allowance. Open out the seams and press along both stitched and unstitched sections. Make two button holes along the straight side of the shorter piece either by hand (see page 37) or by machine.

*step 4*

4 For the side panel, cut a length of fabric twice the circumference of the pillow form by the width of the pad plus ¾" (2 cm) seam allowance all the way around. Fold in and pin pleats approximately 2" (5 cm) wide with a tuck-under of about one-third along the whole length. Check that the pleated side panel fits the circumference of the front panel and adjust if necessary. Secure pleats with basting stitches. Stitch along both sides of the panel, about ½" (1.25 cm) in from the raw edges. With right sides together, stitch short ends together.

*step 6*

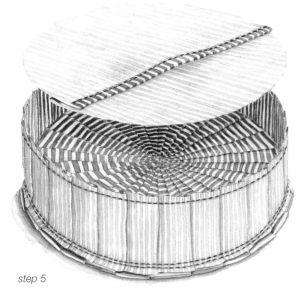

*step 5*

5 To assemble the pillow, place the pleated front and side panels with right sides together. Pin and baste. Stitch with ¾" (2 cm) seam allowance. Repeat to attach back to side panel. Turn right side out. Press. Sew on buttons to line up with each button hole. Insert pillow form.

6 For the rosette, cut four or five circles in graduated sizes, making the largest one big enough to cover all the gathered stitches at the center of the front panel. Sew through the center of each circle, gathering a small amount of fabric to make one or two small overlaps in each. Sew through all the circles to join them through their centers. Using basting stitches, sew the bottom circles to the front panel to secure the rosette.

# box floor cushion

This chunky floor cushion is made from a really strong, robust fabric and a good-quality utilitarian linen dish towel. The thick welting gives the cushion the feeling of an old-fashioned mattress. It will have you, the children and the dog fighting over it!

# box floor cushion

The technique for making this chunky cushion is easy, as the thick welting is actually made like any other welting and stitched into the seams of the cushion. The inner filling could also be made using a sturdy block of foam for greater durability.

1 Using the dish towel or a piece of fabric the same size for the top panel, determine the size of the cushion. Cut a piece of the fabric for the bottom panel to the same size. For the side panel, cut a length of fabric equal to the perimeter of the top by the depth required plus 1" (2.5 cm) seam allowance all the way around. Join pieces together if necessary. For the welting, cut two pieces of fabric to the same length as the side panel by 3" (7.5 cm). Cut two strips of batting to the same length by 1" (2.5 cm).

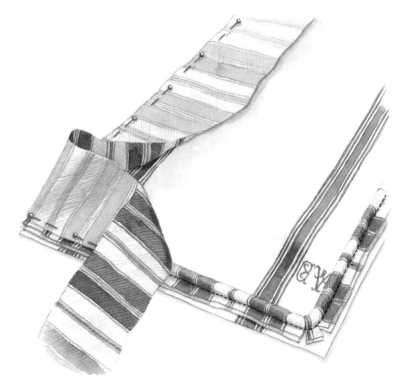

*step 3*

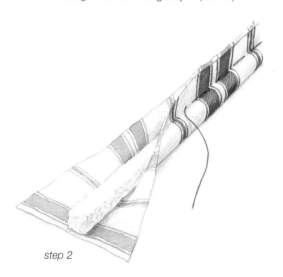

*step 2*

2 To make the welting, lay the narrow lengths of fabric right side down and place a strip of batting along the center of each. Fold fabric in half lengthwise to enclose the batting, aligning the raw edges. Pin and baste down long edge as close as possible to the batting. Stitch.

3 With the top panel right side up, lay the welting all the way around the outer edges, aligning the raw edges. Pin and baste. Place the side panel all the way around the edge of the top panel, again aligning the raw edges and matching any pattern on the side panel to that on the welting. Pin and baste. Stitch as close as possible to the edge of the welting. At each corner, work the stitches in a curve rather than a right angle. Trim the edges and clip the corners.

Fabric panel for
top, such as linen
dish towel

Fabric for bottom,
sides and welting,
such as sturdy linen

Sewing thread

Batting for filling
and welting

4 Join the bottom panel to the side panel in the
same way as for the top, but at one end leave
an opening large enough to insert the padding. Cut
and stack several layers of batting a little thicker
than required and carefully insert them into the
cushion cover. Close the opening using small, neat
slip stitches.

## alternative uses

This type of boxy cushion can be used as more than just a floor cushion. The style
lends itself particularly well to window seats and benches, especially where a more
traditional style is called for. Always use a sturdy fabric like a linen for durability; it
can be checked, striped or printed.

# buttoned pillow sleeve

Heavy cream linen buttoned over delicate toile de Jouy cotton gives a unique and modern feel to pillows. The linen gives the effect of a slipcover for the pillow. Using antique linen for this idea works beautifully, and you can even incorporate a monogram.

# buttoned pillow sleeve

To make this buttoned cover, almost any fabric would be suitable, but the rich and heavy feel of the linen adds some weight. If you have a buttonhole feature on your machine, so much the better, but you can also hand stitch buttonholes using a heavy cotton or linen thread and give the cushion a more original look.

**Materials**

Simple Pillow (see page 12)

Fabric for cover, such as linen

Small amount of fabric to match Simple Pillow, for covered buttons

Sewing thread

Button-covering kit, to make 5 buttons

Buttonhole thread

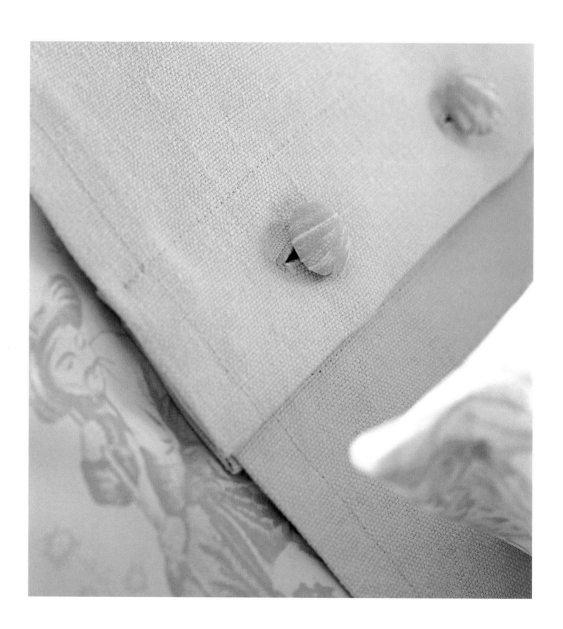

1 Using a soft tape measure, measure around the 'belly' of the Simple Pillow. For the sleeve, cut a piece of fabric 7¼" (18.5 cm) shorter than the length of the Simple Pillow by the belly measurement plus 5" (12.5 cm) seam allowance. Cut five circles of the Simple Pillow fabric for buttons, following the kit instructions.

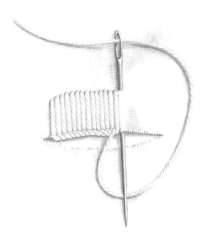

*step 3*

3 To make the buttonholes, measure and mark a line at five evenly spaced points along the center of the turned-in hem ¾" (2 cm) from the edge. Carefully cut buttonholes along the marked lines, ensuring that each is just slightly larger than the diameter of the buttons. Make sure that the button will fit the buttonhole before stitching around the edges of each slit either with the buttonholer on your machine or by hand with buttonhole stitch. To stitch by hand, secure the thread at the end of the slit farthest away from the edge of the fabric. Work evenly spaced buttonhole stitches to the other end of the slit. Work an uneven number of buttonhole stitches of the same length in a semicircle around the end of the slit. Stitch back along the other side of the slit. Finally, work a row of short buttonhole stitches at right angles to the other stitches and fasten off.

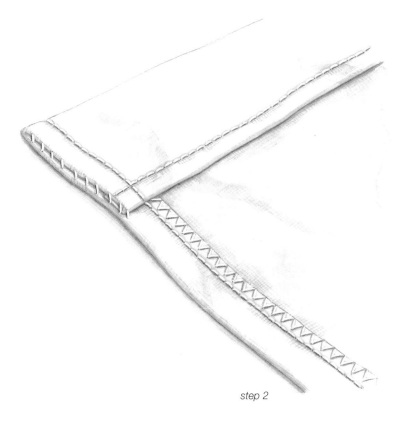

*step 2*

2 Zigzag stitch along both long sides of the cover to prevent fraying. Fold each side in by 1" (2.5 cm) and press. Turn and stitch as close as possible to the zigzagged edges. Zigzag stitch both short ends. Fold each side in by ¼" (0.5 cm) and press. Turn in a further 1½" (3.75 cm) and press. Stitch as close as possible to the turned-in edge. Close the four open sides using small, neat slip stitches.

4 Cover all the buttons with the circles of fabric, following the kit instructions. Sew the buttons onto the corresponding side of the pillow, aligning with the buttonholes. Press. Insert the Simple Pillow and button it up.

# decorated pillows

Embellish a plain pillow with appliqué work to personalize it. Add touches of color, or trim it with strips of decorative or antique ribbon. The heavy red linen would also be perfect for embroidering onto — imagine a cross-stitched monogram in a vibrant orange for a modern interpretation of embroidery.

# ribbon-decorated pillow

**Materials**

Fabric, such as
heavy linen

Decorative ribbon

Sewing thread

Pillow form

There are many wonderful trims and ribbons available today, but many of them
are quite expensive. Used sparingly, they can still make a big impact. Run the
ribbon in even stripes or random patterns, or mix colors — the idea is to make it
your own!

1 For the front panel, cut a piece of fabric to the
size of the pillow form plus ¾" (2 cm) seam
allowance all the way around. For the back panel,
cut a piece of fabric half the width of the pillow form
plus 1¼" (3 cm) on one side and ¾" (2 cm) seam
allowances on the other three sides. Cut another
piece of fabric half with width of the pillow form,
adding 4¾" (12 cm) to the width and a further ¾"
(2 cm) seam allowance on the other three sides.

*step 3*

3 For the ties, cut two strips of fabric 18" (46 cm)
long by 2" (5 cm) wide. Zigzag stitch around
all four sides of each tie to prevent fraying. Turn in
⅜" (1 cm) on both long ends. Press. Stitch. Turn
in ⅜" (1 cm) on both short ends. Press and stitch.

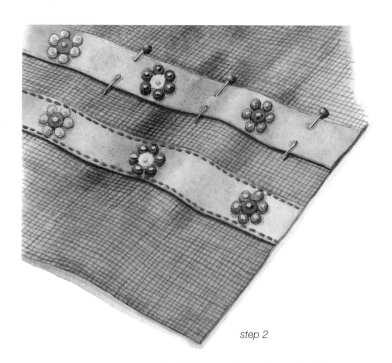

*step 2*

2 Cut four lengths of decorative ribbon to the
same width as the front panel and stitch along
both long edges to secure them.

*step 4*

4 Zigzag stitch around all four sides of the front panel and both back panels. Lay the two back panels right side down. Turn in ¾" (2 cm) on one short side of each. Press. Stitch twice — once near the front fold and once near the zigzagged edge. Take the shorter of the two back panels and with the right side down pin one of the ties in the middle with the end of the tie aligning with the hemmed edge of the panel. Baste, then stitch. Take the wider of the two back pieces and with the right side facing up pin the other tie in the middle with the end 3" (7.5 cm) inside the hemmed edge of the panel. Baste, then stitch just inside the short ends and extending about 1" (2.5 cm) on either side of the long ends.

5 Lay the two back panels with right sides together over the front panel, with raw sides edge to edge so that the two seamed edges overlap by 3½" (9 cm). Pin and baste together ¾" (2 cm) from the edges. Stitch. Turn right side out. Press. Insert the pillow form.

# appliqué-decorated pillow

## Materials

Fabric, such as
heavy linen

Felt in two
contrasting colors

Embroidery floss
in two contrasting
colors to match felt

Sewing thread

Pillow form

Appliqué work is a needlecraft skill that has been used for centuries to personalize textiles. With this strong motif and vibrant colored felt, the traditional detail of handmade French knots looks very contemporary. Felt is a good fabric for appliqué work as it does not fray.

1 Follow all of step 1 as given for Ribbon-decorated Pillow (see page 40).

2 For the appliqué, trace a pattern onto a piece of felt. Carefully cut around the outline. Trace a smaller pattern onto a different color felt. Cut carefully around the outline. Cut out a small circle of the same color felt as the largest appliqué pattern piece. Layer, pin and baste all three pieces of felt to the front panel.

*step 3*

3 Using contrasting embroidery floss, work around the outside edge of the largest piece of felt using evenly spaced French knots (as shown here). Attach the middle and smallest felt pieces in the same way.

4 Proceed as given for Ribbon-decorated Pillow (see page 40).

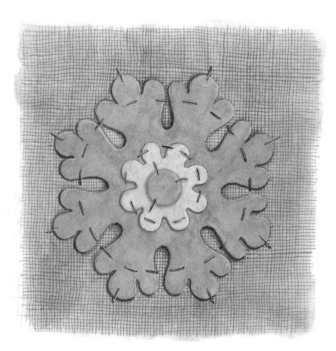

*step 2*

## appliqué work

The great thing about appliqué work is that you can use any design or pattern;
make a paper template to try out the size and shape before you cut the fabric.
Be inspired by nature, or take the pattern from a piece of china or a color
from another fabric in the room. You can use a serger to attach the appliqué to
the pillow, a simple running stitch or even a fusible backing to stick it on; just
remember to use a fabric that is tightly woven to prevent it from looking tattered.

appliqué-decorated pillow    43

drapes

# basic clip-on drapes

For a really quick and easy pair of drapes, it's hard to beat the simplicity of metal drape clips. There are no handmade headings or drape tapes to grapple with. All you need to do is hem each drape all the way around, gather the top into fairly even pleats and attach the clips. Almost any fabric can be used for this method: an antique quilt looks stunning at a window and provides some insulation, too.

# basic clip-on drapes

## Materials

Fabric, such as
lightweight wool

Sewing thread

Drape clips

For a natty pair of instant drapes, cheap red felt and metal clips provide a quick makeover for a window. These drapes can be made entirely by hand if you don't have access to a sewing machine; the instructions below are for this method.

**1** Cut two drops of fabric to the required length plus 8" (20 cm). For the first drape, turn in both sides ½" (1.25 cm), press, then turn in a further 1" (2.5 cm) and press. Pin, baste and slip stitch by hand down both sides. Use small slip stitches to close up both turnovers at either end.

*step 1*

*step 2*

**2** Turn down the top 1" (2.5 cm) and press, then turn down a further 2" (5 cm) and press. Herringbone stitch down by hand. Turn up the bottom 2" (5 cm), press and turn up a further 3" (7.5 cm) and press. Herringbone stitch down by hand and close up the turn-ups at both ends with small, neat slip stitches. To hang, put the clips on the pole and gather up small double pleats for each clip, evenly spaced apart. Repeat for second drape.

Drape clips come in so many guises now, but the basic principle always remains: a clip incorporates a gather in the fabric to give a draped look.

Top left: Hefty wrought iron clips can hold even heavy fabric.

Top right: New magnetic clips are elegant and practical for lighter materials.

Bottom left: Traditional clips, which can be painted.

Bottom right: Contemporary chrome mini-clips are surprisingly sturdy.

# contrast lined drapes

In a bathroom, where light as well as privacy is required, one attractive solution is diaphanous modern lace lined with a thin silk. These layers are sewn together only at the top and are then gathered onto a metal rod with a pocket heading. Light filters through the layers of fabric to give a pretty summery look.

# contrast lined drapes

For this type of window treatment it is important to use two very lightweight fabrics, otherwise the gathering for the pocket heading will look bulky and lumpy. It is also advisable to have the pocket fit the rod quite snugly or it won't gather up as shown in the photograph.

**1** First measure or calculate the circumference of the drape rod. To this measurement add 2" (5 cm) for the heading and pocket plus ½" (1.25 cm) for the hem (call this measurement A). To this add the panel length required from the bottom of the pocket plus 1½" (3.75 cm) for the seam allowance. Cut two panels of this measurement from each of the two fabrics.

**2** On all four panels, turn in ½" (1.25 cm) on each side. Press and turn in a further ½" (1.25 cm). Press, then machine down. For the hems turn up ½" (1.25 cm) and press. Then turn up a further 1" (2.5 cm), press and machine down.

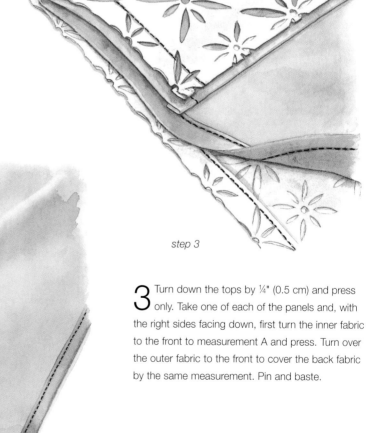

*step 3*

**3** Turn down the tops by ¼" (0.5 cm) and press only. Take one of each of the panels and, with the right sides facing down, first turn the inner fabric to the front to measurement A and press. Turn over the outer fabric to the front to cover the back fabric by the same measurement. Pin and baste.

*step 2*

## Materials

Fabric for front, such
as lightweight
cutwork cotton

Fabric for lining in
contrast color, such
as lightweight silk

Sewing thread

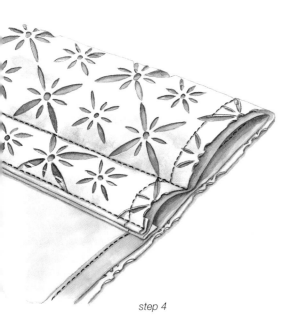

*step 4*

4 Using tailor's chalk and a hard-edged ruler,
draw a line 2" (5 cm) from the top and another
one just above the folded edge. Machine along these
two lines to form the pocket. Thread the rod into the
pocket and gather up the drapes as required.

## alternative fabrics

This laser-cut cotton is a modern-day lace, that instantly portrays a more
contemporary look. Antique lace or a very thin handkerchief linen would also
admit enough light through this type of drape.

# unlined drapes with tape ties

Minimal sewing is required for these smart tailored drapes. All four sides of the drape are edged with woven cotton tape, which is also used for the ties that are attached to the wooden drape rings. The fabric used is a medium-weight linen-and-cotton mixture that hangs well.

# unlined drapes with tape ties

The woven cotton tape not only incorporates the hemming but provides a decorative feature: at the bottom edge of the drapes, an extra band of the tape is sewn horizontally about 10" (25 cm) from the ground. You could use this technique to create stripes of varying widths.

**Materials**

Fabric, such as heavy linen

Cotton tape

Sewing thread

1 Cut two pieces of the fabric to the drop length
required plus 1" (2.5 cm) seam allowance all the
way around. For each drape, cut two lengths of
tape the drop of the drape plus ½" (1.25 cm) and
seven lengths of 30" (76 cm) each for the ties.

2 With the fabric facing right side up, turn
hems to the front 1" (2.5 cm) down both sides
of the drape. Press. For the decorative band at
the bottom of the drape, cut a length of tape to
the width of the drape and lay it approximately 10"
(25 cm) from the bottom. Tuck the tape into the
folded hem at both sides. Trim any excess tape.

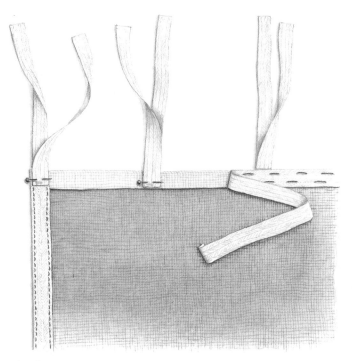

*step 4*

4 For the bottom, lay a piece of the tape along
the bottom edge and turn under ½" (1.25 cm)
on both sides. Pin, baste and machine down along
all edges of the tape. For the ties at the top, turn
under both short ends ¼" (0.5 cm) on each tie,
press and machine down. Fold ties in half and
space evenly along the top about ½" (1.25 cm) from
the top of the folded edge.

5 Lay a length of the tape for the top, close
to the edge and incorporating the ties.
Fold under both ends ¼" (0.5 cm). Pin, baste
and machine down both edges of the tape and
down the short sides.

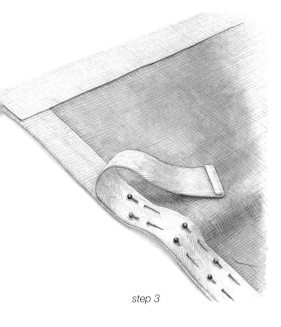

*step 3*

3 Turn down both the top and bottom of the
drape in the same way and press. For the
sides, lay over a length of the tape right to the
edge, and turn under the top and bottom of the
tape ½" (1.25 cm). Pin, baste and machine down
both edges of the tape and along the two short
ends, to incorporate the hem.

# unlined drapes with sewn ties

Make the ties from the same fabric as the drapes, in this case a narrow stripe. The reinforced stitching used to attach the ties — a square box with a crisscross — can be a decorative feature, as it is both strong and attractive. Use a medium-to-heavyweight fabric so that the drapes hang well.

*step 2*

## Materials

Fabric, such as
sturdy striped cotton

Sewing thread

1 Cut two lengths of the fabric the drop required plus 8½" (21.5 cm). Cut seven strips of the same fabric, with the stripe running horizontally, 4" (10 cm) wide by 28" (71 cm) long.

2 Turn in the sides of each drape ½" (1.25 cm) and press. Turn in a further ½" (1.25 cm). Press, pin, baste and machine down. Turn down the top ¾" (2 cm) and press. Turn down a further 1¾" (4.5 cm), press, pin, baste and machine down. Turn up the bottom hem 3" (7.5 cm), press and turn up a further 3" (7.5 cm). Press, pin, baste and machine down.

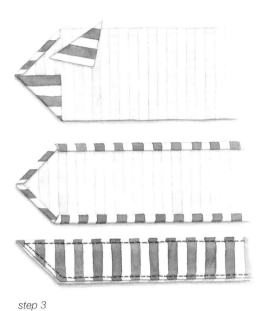

*step 3*

3 For the ties, fold in each corner at a 45-degree angle. Press and trim back the folds to leave ¼" (0.5 cm) seam allowance. Next, fold in ¼" (0.5 cm) down both long edges and press. Fold in half lengthwise and press. Pin, baste and machine down around the perimeter of the tie. Repeat for all ties.

*step 4*

4 With a drape right side down, pin one of the ties to each top outside edge and space the rest evenly. Baste, then machine right through to the front to make the outline of a square, then machine to join opposite corners to form a cross.

# lined drapes with tiebacks

These heavily woven linen drapes, with a soft pink checked lining, have hand-sewn headings. The glimpse of a patterned lining behind the plain drapes is an intriguing design detail — the calmness of the plain outer linen belies the pretty decorative lining. The wide tiebacks are reversible.

# lined drapes with tiebacks

Here the lining fabric and the outer fabric are hemmed and sewn edge to edge before being bagged out, making them much simpler than very formal drapes. Once the 'bag' is turned right side out, it is much easier to put in the pleats.

**Materials**

Fabrics for front and back of drapes and tiebacks, preferably same widths

Sewing thread

Buckram 5" (12.5 cm) deep

Steel hooks

1 Cut three lengths of each fabric to the drop required, adding 8¾" (22 cm) seam allowance. Fold one length of each of the fabrics in half lengthwise, press and cut in half.

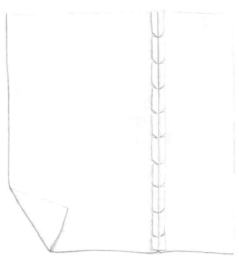

*step 2*

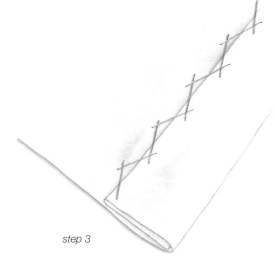

*step 3*

2 To join widths, lay the full drop right side up with the half-width right side down, aligning one side. (Always keep the half-width to the outer edges of each drape.) Pin, baste, then machine ½" (1.25 cm) in from the edges. Snip the selvages at an angle approximately every 4" (10 cm) to release any tension. Iron out the seam flat. Make the second drape in the same way.

3 Turn up the bottom to make a double 4" (10 cm) hem by first ironing in a crease 8" (20 cm) up from the lower edge. Open out and fold in a 4" (10 cm) crease so the raw edge lines up exactly with the first crease. Press. Refold the first crease and herringbone stitch the hem in place. Repeat for both front and back panels of each drape.

Machine the pleat in place from the pin position at the top edge down for 4½" (11.5 cm). Reverse stitch at the end of each fold to secure. Form the rest of the pleats in the same way. Turn each large pleat into a smaller double pleat by opening out the top edge and pushing in another pleat, creasing the buckram firmly to hold the pleat. Using strong thread, hand stitch across the bottom of the front of each pleat to hold. Attach steel drape hooks to the back of each pleat.

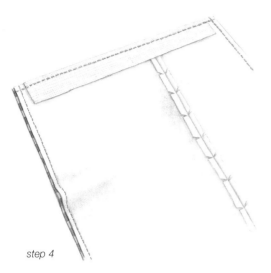

*step 4*

4 Lay out one panel of each fabric with the right sides facing and cut a length of buckram to the width of the drape minus 1½" (3.75 cm). Center the buckram and, aligning it with the top edge, baste in place. Machine the two fabrics and the buckram ¾" (2 cm) down from the top edge. Pin, baste and then machine down both sides, leaving ¾" (2 cm) seam allowance. Turn the drape right side out. Press.

5 For the pleats, work out the finished width required for the drape and subtract this from the width of the flat drape. Divide this by the number of pleats you want and mark the center of each one with a pin at the top of the drape. Pinch together about 1½" (3.75 cm) either side of each pin and crease the buckram firmly along the fold.

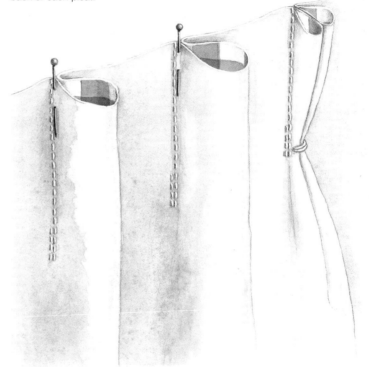

*step 5*

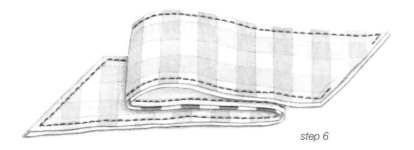

*step 6*

6 Cut two pieces of each of the fabrics 80" (203 cm) long by 11" (28 cm), with all ends at a 45-degree angle. Lay two contrasting pieces right sides together and pin, baste and then machine ¼" (0.5 cm) from the edge, around two long sides, one short side and part of the second short side. Turn right side out and slip stitch the opening. Press.

lined drapes with tiebacks   63

# ruffle-edged drapes

A gorgeous heavy wool needs no lining to provide warmth and insulation on these garden doors. The linen scrim with a silky braid adds a softening decorative touch to the edges. Ordinary heading tape is used for attaching the drapes to the plain metal pole.

# ruffle-edged drapes

## Materials

Wool or tartan fabric

Sewing thread

Linen scrim

Fan edging trim

2" (5 cm) wide
curtain tape

Attaching drape tape to the heading of a drape needs to be done methodically: sew one long edge of the tape going from left to right, then reverse this for the other long edge, so the tension is even.

**1** Cut two lengths of the fabric to the drop required plus 6¾" (17 cm) seam allowances. Cut two lengths of the scrim to one and a half times the drop required by 3½" (9 cm) wide. Cut two lengths of the trim to the drop of the drape exactly.

**2** Lay the fabric right side down and turn in both sides ½" (1.25 cm). Pin, baste and then

machine the outer edge. Pin and baste the leading edge, and slip stitch by hand. Turn down the top ¾" (2 cm), press and herringbone stitch by hand. Lay a length of the drape tape ¼" (0.5 cm) from the top and turn under ½" (1.25 cm) at either end. Pin, baste and machine down along all the edges of the tape.

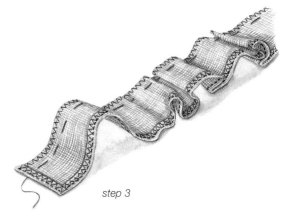

*step 3*

**3** To make the scrim ruffle, zigzag around the perimeter of each strip. Turn in one long edge ¼" (0.5 cm), press and machine down. Turn down both short edges ¼" (0.5 cm), press and machine down. Hand sew a running stitch along the unhemmed long edge and gather to the drop required.

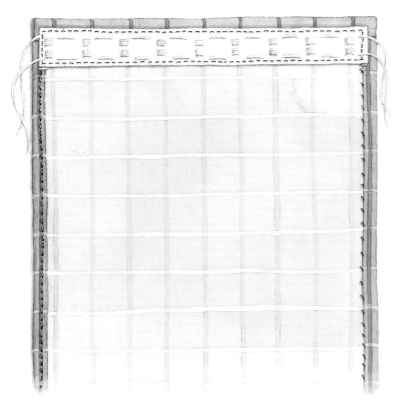

*step 2*

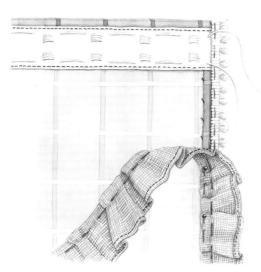

*step 4*

4 Turn up the bottom of the drape 3" (7.5 cm) and press. Turn up another 3" (7.5 cm), press and herringbone stitch by hand. Lay the drape right side down and pin the fan edging along the leading edge of the drape so that only the fan part will be exposed. Pin and baste in place. Lay the gathered length of scrim over this to cover the selvage of the fan edging. Pin, then baste only. Turn the drape right side up and machine down the leading edge to incorporate the fan edging and the scrim.

## alternative edgings

Try other ideas for drape edgings, such as a gathered satin ribbon, glass beading or ruched fringing. Any of these, or a combination, would work well with a fabric like wool to give a contrast of texture and to keep out the light.

# semi-sheer window panels

Cool, calm and collected, this window treatment serves many purposes. The swing-arm pole, or portière rod, lets you control the opening. The sheer upper panels allow light to flood in yet afford privacy, while the opaque lower panels add texture and color. This is a modern take on window treatment using a minimal amount of fabric.

# semi-sheer window panels

**Materials**

Sheer fabric

Heavier linen

Sewing thread

Because the panels will be seen from both the front and back when the portière rods are opened, the fabrics are joined using a French seam – an invisible seam that shows no raw edges.

1 Cut two pieces of the sheer fabric to the drop required plus 3" (7.5 cm) for seam allowances and the pocket heading by the width required plus ¾" (2 cm) for each side hem. Cut two pieces of the heavier linen to the drop required plus 1¾" (4.5 cm) for seam allowances by the width required plus ¾" (2 cm) for each side hem.

Pin, baste and machine ⅜" (1 cm) from the edge, securing the ends of the seam by backstitching with the machine. Trim back the seam allowance to ¼" (0.5 cm). Turn the fabric right sides together and press so that the machined line is right at the edge. Baste, then machine ⅜" (1 cm) from the edge. Open out and press the seam to one side.

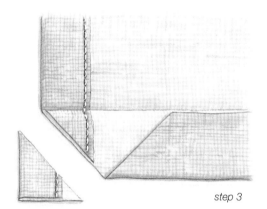

*step 3*

3 Turn in the sides ⅜" (1 cm) and press. Then turn in a further ⅜" (1 cm), press, baste and machine down. Turn up the bottom ½" (1.25 cm) and press. Then turn up a further ½" (1.25 cm) and press. For a mitered corner, open out and fold the corner in at a 45-degree angle and press. Open this out and cut back the fabric to the fold mark of the triangle. Fold the two creases back up. Pin, baste and machine down.

*step 2*

2 Join the sheer and linen fabrics using a French seam to conceal the join. Lay the pieces right sides facing and lined up where they are to join.

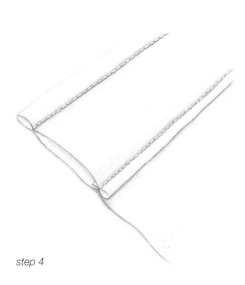

*step 4*

4 For the top, fold down the sheer ½" (1.25 cm) and press. Fold down a further 2½" (6.5 cm) and press. Using tailor's chalk and a ruler, draw two lines, one ½" (1.25 cm) and the other 1¾" (4.5 cm) from the top. Machine along the two lines to form the pocket.

*step 5*

5 Portière rods are useful in many circumstances: dormer and casement windows, over doors as draft protectors and even on windows where there is limited room. Once the portière rod is fixed in place, slip the pocket of the panel over the arm.

semi-sheer window panels    71

# simple swag

The practical and decorative uses of a simple swag are many: the drape of the fabric can soften the hard lines of an austere window, add color and texture, hide ugly roller-blind fixings or add height to a window. This strong yellow linen is edged with a charming gingham ribbon.

# simple swag

**Materials**

Wooden batten

Fabric

Sewing thread

Ribbon for edge

Contrast fabric for ties

Strong cotton thread

It is best to use a loosely woven fabric such as linen, raw silk or soft muslin, as they will have better draping qualities than other textiles. Putting in the folds can be somewhat awkward, but a little perseverance usually pays off.

**1** Cut a piece of batten to slightly wider than the frame of the window, and cover all over with the same fabric as the swag, using a staple gun to fix in place. Attach this batten just over the top of the window. Cut a piece of the fabric the width of the window plus about 20" (50 cm) either side for the tails to hang down, by a drop of about 45" (115 cm).

**3** For the ties, cut two strips of the contrast fabric 8" (20 cm) long by 4½" (11.5 cm) wide. Fold in half lengthwise with right sides facing and press. Machine around two long and one short side ½" (1.25 cm) from the edges. Turn right side out. Fold in the remaining raw edges ½" (1.25 cm) and machine closed. Press.

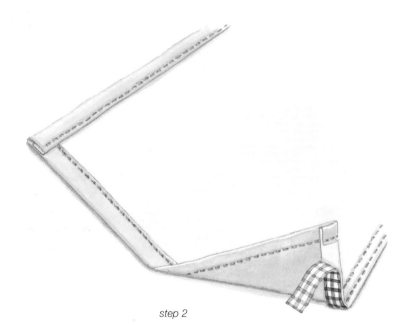

*step 2*

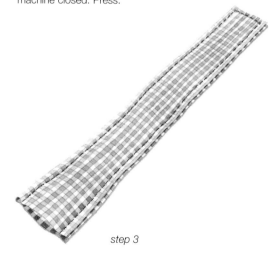

*step 3*

**2** Turn in both ends ⅜" (1 cm) twice to make a double hem. Press, pin, baste and machine down. Do the same for one of the long edges. For the remaining raw edge, turn up a ⅜" (1 cm) hem and press. Over this pin a length of the ribbon to cover the raw edges, pin, baste and machine down.

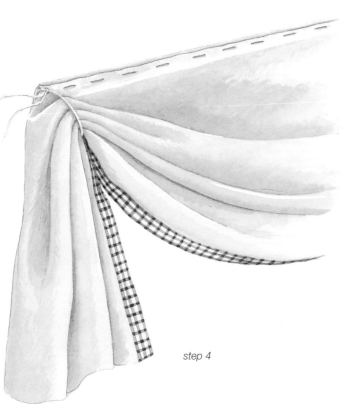

4 To fix the swag, find the middle of it and, using a staple gun, staple it straight onto the top of the fabric-covered batten. Continue stapling out to each corner. Gather the loose fabric into folds at one end, making a series of neat pleats at the side. Secure this using strong cotton thread tied in a knot. Fold the other side in the same way. Wrap the ties over the gathered ends and secure with a couple of staples.

*step 4*

simple swag

# unlined roman blind

The clean lines of a Roman shade work well in both traditional and contemporary interiors. Roman shades are unfussy and require only a minimum of fabric. This deeply pleated, unlined shade is made from thin linen to which a monogram has been embroidered. It filters the light to give a soft effect.

# unlined roman blind

**Materials**

Wooden batten

Length of linen with
neat selvages

Velcro tape cut
to the width of
the window

3 x screw eyes

Sewing thread

6 x Roman blind rings

3 x thin wooden
dowels, width of blind

Cleat

Window blind cord

The narrow red lines along the selvages of this antique linen looked so smart that I decided to incorporate them into the blind. If you can't find anything similar and need to add a hem to each side, turn in both sides of the fabric ½" (1.25 cm) twice, press and machine.

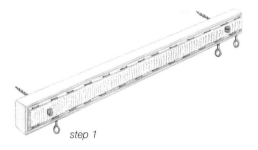

*step 1*

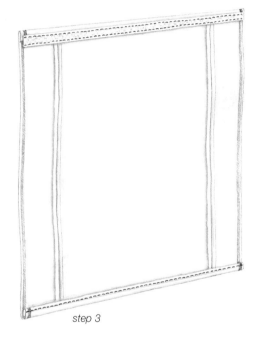

*step 3*

1 Cut a wooden batten the width of the window and cover with fabric, using a staple gun. Staple the hook side of the piece of Velcro tape to the front of the batten. Attach two screw eyelets to the bottom of the batten 6" (15 cm) from each side, and one on the same end you intend to put the cleat. Attach the batten to the frame of the window.

2 If the fabric width is the same as the window, so much the better. If not, add widths to either side, incorporating the woven selvages (in this case the red edge of the linen), so you end up with a piece of linen the width required plus 4½" (11.5 cm) for dowels and 1" (2.5 cm) for hems.

3 For the top, turn down the linen ½" (1.25 cm) and press. Machine the fluffy side of the Velcro tape to cover the raw edge. For the bottom hem turn up ½" (1.25 cm) and press. Then turn up a further ½" (1.25 cm). Press, baste and machine down.

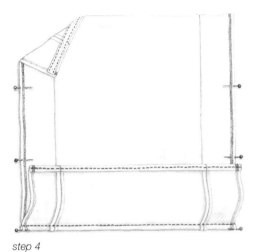

*step 4*

4 With the panel right side up, divide it into four equal sections and mark with pins. This is where the three pleats will be made. Fold up the linen at the first pins and press. Using tailor's chalk and a hard-edged ruler draw a line ¾" (2 cm) from the fold. Machine along this line to form the first pocket. Repeat for the other two pockets. Sew two Roman blind rings onto the back of each pleat 6" (15 cm) in from the sides. Insert the dowels into the pockets.

*step 5*

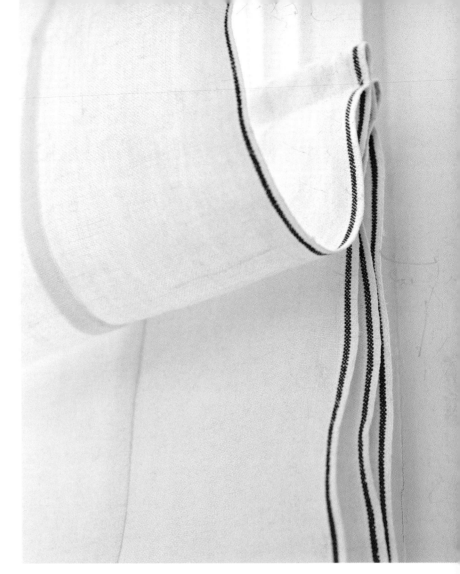

5 Fix the cleat to the side of the window. To string the blind, cut two lengths of window blind cord three times the drop of the blind. Working on the back of the blind and starting with the vertical row that is the farthest from the cleat side, knot the cord to the bottom ring, using a double knot. String the cord through the two other rings. Repeat for the other side. Now attach the blind to the fabric-covered batten. Run the blind cord through the screw eyelets so that they meet on the cleat side. Pull the two cords to pull up the pleats and ensure they are straight by adjusting the cord. Tie into a knot at the end and attach to the cleat.

# lined roman blind

Instead of the more usual vertical stripes used in window treatments, try a horizontal stripe for a change. With the pleats of the blind, it makes a window look wider and rather elegant.

# lined roman blind

## Materials

Wooden batten

Fabric for blind

Velcro tape cut to the
width of the window

4 x screw eyelets

Antique monogram

Sewing thread

Cotton lining fabric,
such as cotton
gingham

9 x Roman
blind rings

4 x thin wooden
dowels

Cleat

Window
blind cord

The technique for this lined Roman blind is very similar to the unlined version.
The main difference is that here the pockets are at the front and the blind is lined
with contrasting red gingham, which looks fresh and inviting from the street, too!

1 Prepare a fabric-covered wooden batten
as in step 1 of the Unlined Roman Blind
(see page 78), but add a third screw eyelet in
the middle for extra support.

Place the fabrics right sides together and pin,
baste, then machine ½" (1.25 cm) in from the two
sides and bottom. Turn right side out and press.

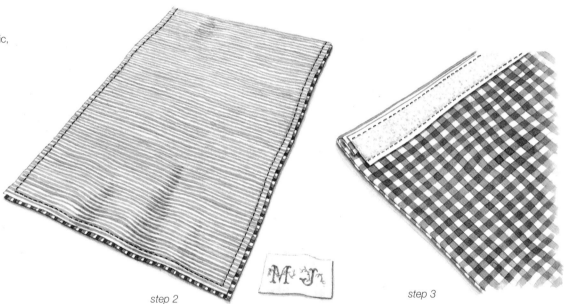

*step 2*

*step 3*

2 Cut a piece of both the fabric and the lining
to the drop required, plus 6" (15 cm) (for four
dowels) and 1" (2.5 cm) seam allowance, by the
width required, plus 1" (2.5 cm) seam allowance
on both sides. Cut out the monogram. Turn under
¼" (0.5 cm) all around and press.

3 Lay the blind right side down, turn down the
top ½" (1.25 cm) and press. Pin the fluffy side
of the Velcro tape to the top of the fabric. Baste
and machine down.

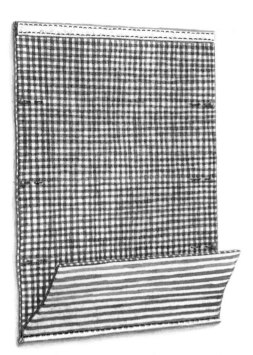

*step 4*

4 With the right side facing down, divide the length of the shade into five equal sections, and mark each side with pins. Fold up the blind at the first set of pins and press. Using tailor's chalk and a hard-edged ruler draw a line ¾" (2 cm) from the crease and machine down to create a pocket. Repeat for the rest of the pockets. These pockets are at the front of the blind, so with the blind still right side down, sew three rows of rings to the back of each pleat, 6" (15 cm) from each side and one in the middle. Insert the dowels into the pockets. Pin the monogram to the blind and, using small slip stitches, hand sew to the front fabric only. Follow the instructions for stringing the blind as in Unlined Roman Blind (see page 79).

## adding a monogram

Old linens often yield monograms that can be cut out as patches and appliquéd to the front of drapes and shades, either by hand, using embroidery floss and blanket stitch, or with a serger on the sewing machine. Hand embroidering a monogram is also special; use embroidery floss and work it in cross stitch or back stitch.

# swedish roll-up blind

Used for centuries all over Sweden, blinds like this one are easy to make and easy to use. Traditionally they are made from a single layer of woven linen that is reversible, as you can see the back when they are rolled up. The glass rings let the cord glide through smoothly for opening and closing. This blind is backed in simple gingham to provide a contrast to the floral fabric.

# swedish roll-up blind

## Materials

Fabric for front, such as lightweight cotton

Contrast fabric for back

Sewing thread

½" (1.25 cm) wooden dowel ¼" (0.5 cm) narrower than width of blind, ends covered in the fabric

Wooden batten ¼" (0.5 cm) narrower than blind, covered in same fabric as back of blind

2 x glass rings

Blind cord

Cleat

It is better to use two fabrics of the same weight for this blind, so it will glide smoothly. The fabrics need to be perfectly aligned and pressed to prevent any wrinkling once the blind is up.

1 Cut a piece of each of the two fabrics the width of the blind plus ¾" (2 cm) by the drop required plus 3½" (9 cm). Cut two pieces of the fabric for the front panel 9" (23 cm) long by 3" (7.5 cm) wide for the ties. Place the large front and back pieces edge to edge and right sides facing. Pin, baste and machine the two sides and bottom, ⅜" (1 cm) from the edges. Turn right side out and press. Now top stitch the blind by machining down very close to the edge on the two sides and bottom. Baste the wooden dowel to the bottom of the front of the blind to hold in place.

*step 2*

2 For the ties to hold the glass rings, fold a strip in half lengthwise, right sides facing, and press. Pin, baste and machine ¼" (0.5 cm) from the edges on the long side. Turn right side out and press.

3 Staple the top of the blind to the back of the batten. Fold the ties in half and slip through a glass ring on each, then staple the raw edges to the back of the batten, about 7" (17.75 cm) from each side. Cut two lengths of blind cord about three times the drop of the blind. Knot one end of one cord and staple to the back of the batten in the middle of the tie. Repeat for the other. Attach the cleat. Put up the batten, being careful to use an awl to make holes in the fabric covering the batten so as not to twist it. Roll up the blind to the front,

*step 1*

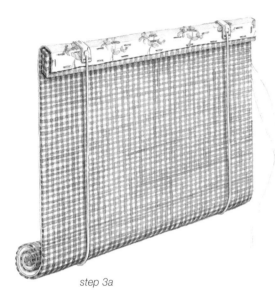

*step 3a*

enclosing the dowel, and bring around the first piece of cord and thread it through the glass ring above it. Repeat for the other cord. Thread the cord farthest away from the cleat end through the next glass ring. Pull the cords gently until the blind rolls up easily, and knot off.

*step 3b*

## matching fabrics

-------------------------------------

When teaming two patterns, remember that one must always be a foil for the other. A floral print almost always looks good when teamed with a check or a stripe that picks up one of the colors. Neither the color nor the scale of the foil should overwhelm the color and pattern of the floral. If in doubt, remember that most patterns look great backed with a plain white or cream linen.

bed lin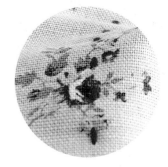en

# lace-edged coverlet

With all the gorgeous double cloth and matelassé fabrics now on the market, let alone the array of vintage textiles, you can easily transform a bed with a custom-made coverlet. Rummaging at antique sales for a length of vintage lace or old silk ribbon can provide the inspiration for endless sewing ideas.

# lace-edged coverlet

**Materials**

Matelassé cotton
fabric

Antique cotton lace

Sewing thread

Velvet ribbon

Washing and preshrinking all the components of this bedspread will make it not only look elegant but also be practical. The lace is machined to the matelassé fabric and the velvet ribbon is neatly hand sewn to hide the machine stitches.

1 Cut a piece of matelassé cotton fabric to the size required plus an extra ¾" (2 cm) seam allowance all the way around. (Join widths if necessary.) Cut a length of lace long enough to go all the way around the outside edge of the matelassé cotton, plus 1" (2.5 cm) for each corner to pleat. With the matelassé cotton facing right side down, turn in both long sides 1" (2.5 cm) and press, baste and tack. Repeat for the two shorter sides. Pin the lace right side down and facing out over the folded edges, making a small pleat at each corner. Baste and stitch down to incorporate turned-in seams.

*step 2*

2 Cut a length of velvet ribbon slightly longer than the perimeter of the bedspread. Using tiny slip stitches, hand sew both edges of the ribbon to cover the join of the lace and the matelassé cotton, mitering the corners (see page 70).

*step 1*

## choosing fabrics

The best way to narrow your search for fabric is to choose a good texture and look for colors that will suit the room or simply for colors that you love. This can include anything from a vintage quilt to the most high-tech double-woven cloth. Choose trims to enhance the fabric, pulling out a color, introducing a new texture or creating a pattern (see Ribbon-decorated Coverlet on page 94).

# ribbon-decorated coverlet

**Materials**

Matelassé cotton
fabric

A selection of ribbons
and tapes

Sewing thread

The simplest quilted cotton bedspread can be totally transformed by adding randomly spaced strips of assorted ribbon. Suddenly there is a sophisticated and modern feel to the bedspread, which you've achieved with great ease and very little expense.

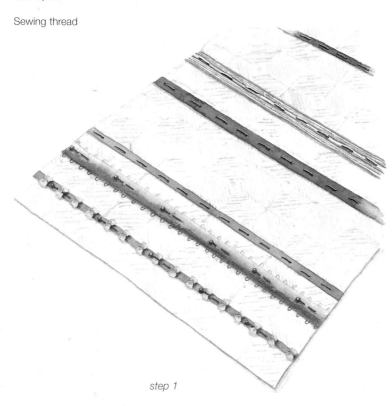

*step 1*

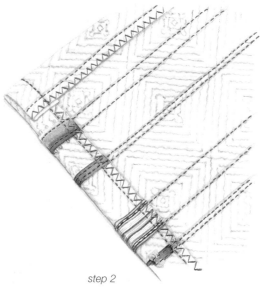

*step 2*

2 Zigzag stitch all the way around the perimeter of the matelassé cotton to prevent fraying, catching in the ends of the ribbon. Lay the cotton right side down and turn in both long sides 2" (5 cm). Press, baste and stitch. Repeat for the two shorter sides, keeping the corners crisp and neat.

1 Cut a piece of matelassé cotton fabric to the size required plus an extra 2" (5 cm) seam allowance all the way around. (Join widths if necessary.) Cut lengths of the various ribbons and tapes to the same width as the matelassé cotton. Lay the matelassé cotton right side up and pin the ribbons and tapes across the width of the bedspread to form random stripes. Baste, then stitch each one down along both sides to secure.

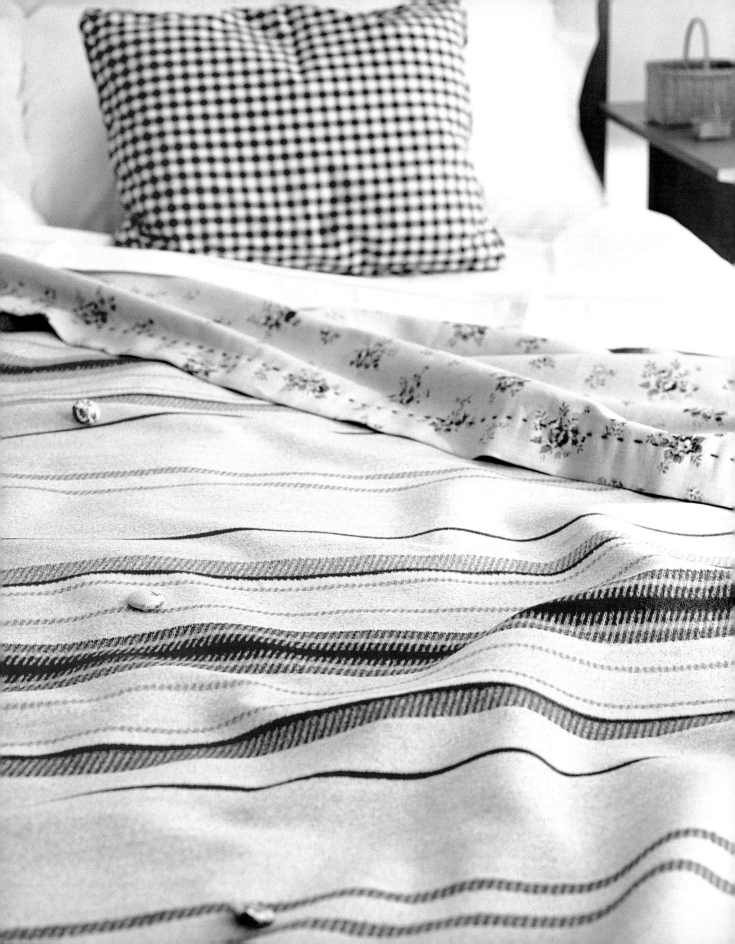

# linen-backed wool bedspread

Lightweight wool, backed with a fresh summery linen print, gives this bedspread a dual life: the warmth of the wool looks cozy for the winter months, while for summer you can use the reverse side in cool linen for a crisper style. The hand-stitched border gives the bedspread a custom-made look that is easy to achieve.

# linen-backed wool bedspread

**Materials**

Wool fabric

Linen fabric

Embroidery floss

Button-covering kit
for 6 buttons

6 x small shirt
buttons for back

Sewing thread

To prevent the two fabrics from sliding around, anchor them at regular intervals with covered buttons on one side and small shirt buttons on the other. Use a chunky embroidery floss for the hand-stitched border and make sure the color visually enhances or ties together both fabrics.

1 Cut a piece of wool to the size required. Cut a piece of linen to the same size as the wool plus an extra 2½" (6.5 cm) all the way around for the turnover. Turn in ¾" (2 cm) on both long sides of the linen and press. Turn in ¾" (2 cm) on the other two sides of the linen and press. Turn in a further 1¾" (4.5 cm) on both long sides of the linen and press. Turn in ¾" (2 cm) on the other two sides of the linen and press. Open out the second folds and place the wool into the creases, right side up.

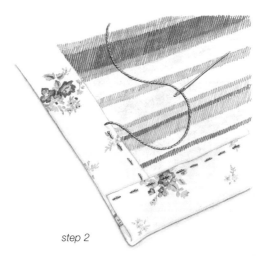

*step 2*

2 Bring over the folded edges, pin and baste. Using embroidery floss, secure the two fabrics together with a running stitch all the way around.

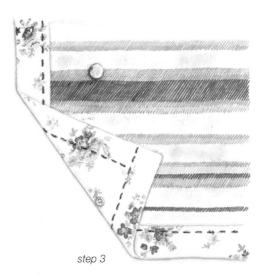

*step 3*

3 Cover six buttons with the linen, following the kit manufacturer's instructions. Position the buttons evenly on the wool side of the bedspread and pin into place. Sew on each button, attaching it to a shirt button on the floral side to anchor it.

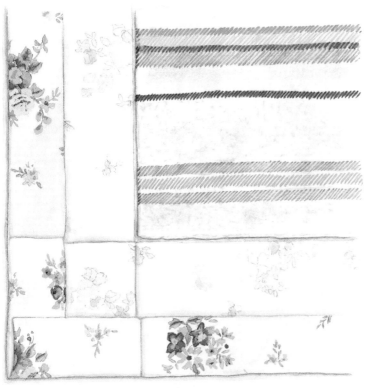

*step 1*

linen-backed wool bedspread    **99**

# fleece throw with pompoms

**Materials**

Thick fleece

Tapestry wool

Thick card

Sewing thread

This fun fleece throw with big woolen pompoms adds a touch of joy and flair to any bedroom. The contrasting blanket-stitched edges give a tailored finish to the fleece. This project would make a wonderful wedding present.

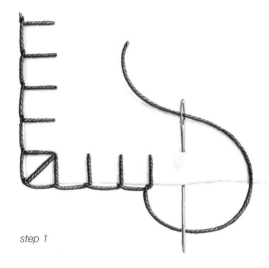

*step 1*

*step 2*

1 Cut the fleece to the size required. Using the tapestry wool, sew large blanket stitches evenly all the way around the perimeter of the fleece.

2 To make the pompoms, cut two circles from the card about 4" (10 cm) in diameter. Into each card circle cut another circle about 1¾" (4.5 cm) in diameter to form a ring. Cut a 6" (15 cm) length of wool for tying the pompom later and insert it between the card rings, avoiding the center hole. With the card rings together, wrap the wool around the rings until they are covered by two thicknesses of wool all the way around. Slip a pair of scissors between the card rings and snip the wool all the way around. Tighten the tying wool around the pompom and carefully remove it from the rings. Tie the tying wool to secure. Make several pompoms in this way and hand stitch them to the top of the fleece.

# ruffle-edged eiderdown

There is a lovely nostalgic English country-house look to an eiderdown. The combination of a flowery chintz, backed with a rough linen gingham, and the puffy thickness of the squares gives this cover a warm, wintry feeling. It is still possible to find well-worn old eiderdowns in antique markets, but your favorite fabrics and colors will add a special touch.

# ruffle-edged eiderdown

Making this eiderdown yourself requires some sewing experience. Keeping together all the various layers and squares is quite tricky, but it's well worth the effort. There are some companies that will make them for you. For the ultimate in eiderdown luxury, use goose-down fillers (see pages 184–87 for suppliers).

**1** Cut a piece of the cotton fabric for the top to the size required, adding 2½" (6.5 cm) all around for each square (allowance for the quilting), plus an extra ¾" (2 cm) seam allowance all the way around. Cut a piece of the cotton fabric for the bottom and several layers of batting to the same size. (Join widths if necessary.) Cut 4¾" (12 cm) wide strips of the cotton fabric for the ruffle and join to make one long strip twice the perimeter of the eiderdown.

*step 2*

**2** Fold the ruffle in half lengthwise with right sides out and press. Sew two rows of running stitch ⅝" (1.5 cm) from the raw edge. Pull the threads at each end to make even gathers until the frill is the same length as the perimeter of the eiderdown.

step 3

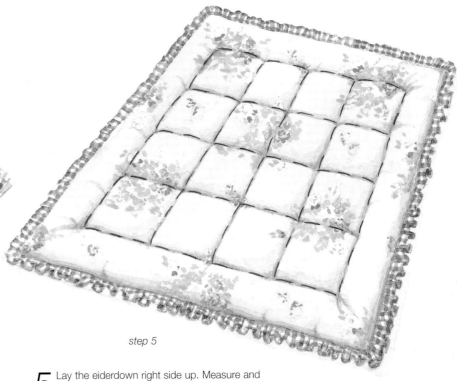

step 5

3 Lay the backing fabric right side up and place the ruffle around the perimeter, ³⁄₁₆" (0.5 cm) in from the outside edge, aligning raw edges. Pin, baste and stitch ³⁄₈" (1 cm) in from the outside edge. Turn backing fabric over and press ruffle to outside.

5 Lay the eiderdown right side up. Measure and mark out an outside border. Measure and mark out equal intervals along this outline to make a grid of squares. Pin, baste and stitch.

step 4

step 6

4 Turn under and press ³⁄₈" (1 cm) all the way around the cotton fabric for the top. Baste. Lay the backing fabric right side down and place several layers of batting on top, followed by the cotton fabric for the top. Pin and baste layers together all the way around, close to each edge.

6 To finish, hand stitch the top fabric to the ruffle, using tiny slip stitches.

## Materials

Cotton fabric, such as glazed cotton chintz, for the top

Cotton fabric, such as gingham, for bottom and frill

Enough batting to make three or four layers

Sewing thread

# patchwork throw

If you, like many people, hoard scraps of leftover fabric or, like me, collect antique textiles, this is the perfect solution for their practical use. Theme them by color, texture or pattern and transform them into an heirloom quilt. This one, which is trimmed with a rich navy cotton velvet, was made for a very special person's 21st birthday.

# patchwork throw

**Materials**

Mixture of colored
linens and cottons,
old and new

Sewing thread

Velvet for edging

Lining fabric for
backing (for a double
bed you will need
80"/200 cm fabric,
59"/150 cm wide)

This bedspread was made using mainly antique textiles, with just a few new ones thrown in. It is important that all the patches are prewashed to prevent any future shrinkage. It also helps if the weight and weave of the patches are similar — mixing a loosely woven linen with a tightly woven cotton will create distortion.

**1** Cut out enough fabric patches of the same length but varying widths to make the size of throw required. Lay the patches out randomly in strips to give an idea of how the finished throw will look.

**2** Starting with the first row, pin, then baste the patches together with a ⅜" (1 cm) seam allowance. Stitch. Press seams out flat. Repeat for each subsequent row. Pin, then baste the strips of patches together, also with a ⅜" (1 cm) seam allowance. Stitch. Press seams out flat.

*step 3*

**3** For the edging, cut strips of velvet across the grain, 2" (5 cm) wide. With right sides together, stitch with ⅜" (1 cm) seams to make a continuous length.

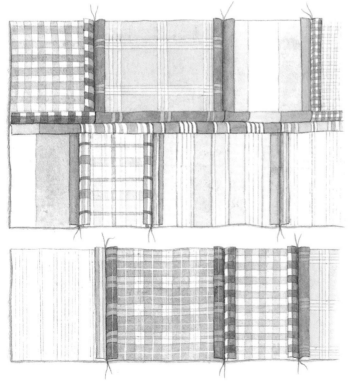

*step 2*

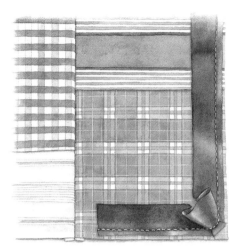

*step 4*

4 With right sides together, lay the velvet strip around the edge of the patchwork throw with raw sides edge to edge. Pin and baste into place, pleating the velvet at the corners. Stitch ⅜" (1 cm) from the edge.

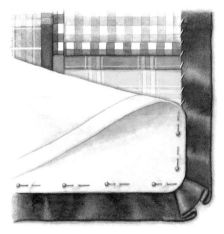

*step 5*

5 Bring the velvet edging around to the reverse side of the throw, turning under ⅜" (1 cm). Pin and hand sew into place. Cut the lining fabric to the size of the throw, adding ⅜" (1 cm) seam allowance all the way around. Turn under ⅜" (1 cm), press and hand sew the lining to the throw.

## choosing fabrics

For any patchwork project the most important factor is to make sure all the patches, be they old or new or a combination, are similar weights and types of fabric. Mixing a wool with a thin cotton creates tension and cleaning problems, so stick with compatible textiles. Always prewash and iron patches before sewing, so that any shrinkage can happen at this stage.

# crib quilt with embroidered initial

The softness of an antique linen makes a tactile and cuddly quilt for a baby or a toddler. A patchwork of assorted linen scraps forms the basis for this quilt, which is then oversewn with a contrasting herringbone stitch. The edges are hand sewn with a simple running stitch in the same embroidery thread. To personalize the quilt, hand embroider one of the patches with an initial.

# crib quilt with embroidered initial

## Materials

35 x 7" (18 cm) squares of antique linen scraps

Sewing thread

Two shades of lavender embroidery floss

Cream linen for backing

The design of this little crib quilt is so simple that you need only the most rudimentary of sewing skills. The charm of this piece is in the embroidery and the mixture of antique cream and ivory linens.

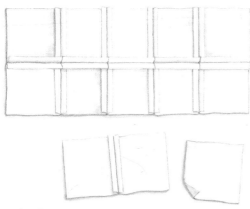

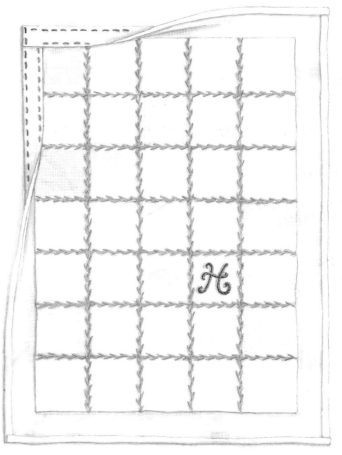

*step 3*

*step 1*

1 Lay out the linen patches into seven rows of five squares. Starting with the top row, pin, then baste the squares together with a ⅜" (1 cm) seam allowance. Stitch. Press seams out flat. Repeat for each row. Pin, then baste the strips of sewn squares together, also with a ⅜" (1 cm) seam allowance. Stitch. Press seams out flat.

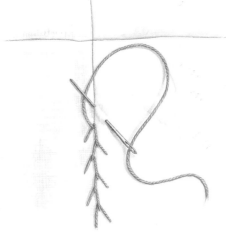

*step 2*

2 Using the embroidery floss, work vertical rows of large feather stitches. Embroider the horizontal rows with the same stitch until all the patchwork seams are concealed. Using the darker floss, embroider a large initial onto one square.

3 Cut a large piece of linen the same size as the patchwork plus an extra 4" (10 cm) all the way around for the border. Lay the linen backing right side down, turn in ⅝" (1.5 cm) on the two longer sides and press. Turn in ⅝" (1.5 cm) on the other two sides and press. Place the patchwork on the linen backing, making sure it is centered. Fold in the two long sides to just cover the patchwork edges. Pin and baste in place. Fold in the top and bottom in the same way. Pin and baste. Using embroidery floss, work a row of running stitches around the inside and outside edges of the border to secure the patchwork. Press.

# tailored bed linen

Admittedly, there is a plethora of bed linen on the market, but sometimes the perfect thing is just elusive: the color may be wrong or the texture too rough. The very fine handkerchief linen used for this duvet cover with its matching pillowcases is of the very highest quality, so it will last for years and years. The simple shapes are trimmed with rickrack.

# duvet cover and pillowcases

**Materials**

Extra-wide linen
or cotton

Rickrack

Sewing thread

Snap fasteners

Many textile companies now offer extra-wide fabrics, which are perfect for making bed linen. This finely woven ivory linen was prewashed to prevent future shrinking. You could substitute most other trims for the rickrack, as long as they are colorfast.

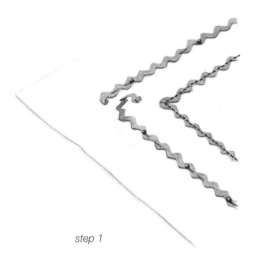

*step 1*

1 Cut two pieces of linen or cotton to the width
and length of the duvet plus an extra ⅝" (1.5 cm)
seam allowance all the way around. Cut another
piece to the width of the duvet plus 1" (2.5 cm) by 8"
(20 cm) for the envelope closure. Cut two lengths of
rickrack to the size of the top panel. Pin, baste and
stitch the rickrack to the top panel, turning under the
two raw edges of the rickrack where they meet.

*step 2*

2 Take the short piece of fabric for the envelope
closure and turn down a double ⅝" (1.5 cm)
hem. Press, pin, baste and stitch. Take the back
panel of the duvet cover and, with the right side
down, turn down 1" (2.5 cm) twice to make a hem
along the width of it. Pin, baste and stitch.

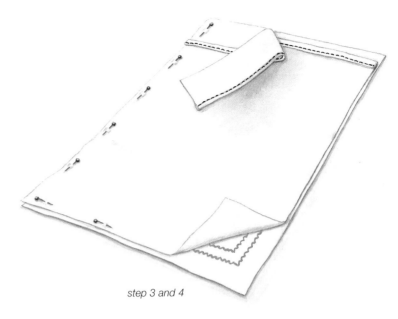

*step 3 and 4*

3 Lay the top panel with the rickrack right side
up and lay the back piece right side down,
aligning the three raw edges. The hemmed edge
will come slightly short of the piece trimmed with
rickrack (by 2"/5 cm). Pin and baste ⅝" (1.5 cm)
from the three raw edges.

4 Keeping the two layers right sides together,
lay the short piece over the envelope end,
aligning the raw edges and with the hemmed seam
right side up. Pin, baste and stitch ⅝" (1.5 cm) from
the edge around the four sides of the duvet cover.
Turn right side out. Attach snap fasteners along
both edges of the opening. Press.

## matching pillowcases

For the pillowcase with the edge of the rickrack peeping out, follow the
instructions for the Simple Pillow on page 12, adding the rickrack as shown
on page 15. Alter the size to suit.

For the pillowcase with the rickrack running down two sides, follow the
instructions for the Simple Pillow, but before going to step 2, pin, baste and
stitch the two strips of rickrack to the front piece of the pillowcase on the right
side. Proceed to step 2.

# tailored dust ruffle

This dust ruffle requires some sewing experience, as a good degree of accuracy is needed for the very tailored finish. For a less-experienced sewer it would be easier to make this using a plain fabric, so the pattern doesn't need to be lined up.

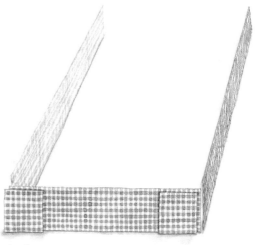

*step 1*

1 The skirt is made from five pieces of fabric. Cut two side panels of cotton to the length of the bed plus 6" (15 cm). Cut an end panel of cotton to the width of the bed base plus 12" (30.5 cm). Add 1⅜" (3.5 cm) seam allowance to the length. Cut two pieces of cotton for the pleats, each 12" (30.5 cm) long and equal to the height of the side and end panels.

2 For the center panel, cut a piece of lining fabric to the length and width of the bed less 12" (30.5 cm). Cut two 6⅝" (17 cm) wide strips of the cotton fabric and the same length as the bed plus 22" (56 cm) and two strips 6⅝" (17 cm) wide and equal to the width of the bed plus 2" (5 cm).

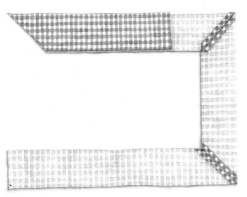

*step 3*

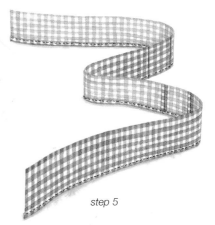

*step 5*

## Materials

Medium-weight cotton, such as gingham

Sewing thread

Thin piping cord

Lining fabric

3 For the central panel, with right sides facing, place a long strip and a short strip together, with raw edges aligning. Pin and baste together at a 45-degree angle diagonally from the top corner. Machine down, stopping ⅝" (1.5 cm) from bottom edge of strip. Attach other strips in the same way until you have a frame. Cut back excess fabric at joins to leave ⅝" (1.5 cm) seams, and press open. Then press in a ⅝" (1.5 cm) fold to the wrong side all around inside edge of border.

5 Take the three pieces of fabric for the skirt and the two pieces for the inverted pleats, and with the right sides together, join one side of each corner pleat to a side panel, then the other side of each corner pleat to the end panel. Pin, baste and machine. Turn up a double ³⁄₁₆" (0.5 cm) hem at the bottom and press. Pin, baste and machine down.

*step 4*

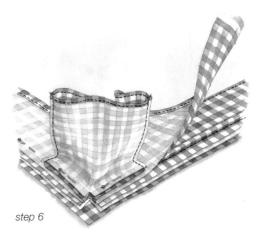

*step 6*

4 Place the center lining panel right side up and lay the frame over it, right side up, making sure it overlaps evenly. Pin, baste and machine the border to the center panel. At the top end of the panel (the headboard end) press in a double ⅜" (1 cm) hem.

6 Cover a length of piping cord with fabric so it is long enough to go around the two sides and end of the bed. Place the center panel right side up and pin the welting around the three unhemmed sides, raw edges together. Place the skirt over the center panel, right side down, raw edges facing out, and align the pleats at the corners. Pin, baste and then machine together ⅝" (1.5 cm) from the edges, keeping the piping cord to the inside of the stitching. Press.

# table linen

# scallop-edged tablecloth

The fresh, crisp quality of gingham is hard to beat in looks, practicality and price. Make a cloth to fit your dining or picnic table and add a decorative scalloped edge. Team the tablecloth with some gingham napkins finished with a velvet ribbon or a rickrack border to complete the look.

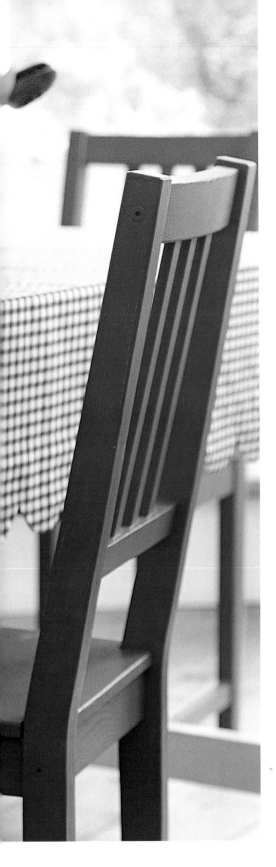

# scallop-edged tablecloth

The secret to the success of this tablecloth is in working out the scallops really accurately, especially at the corners. Adjust your template to suit and remember that the corner scallops could be a little bigger if it helps with the measurements.

## Materials

Lightweight cotton fabric, such as gingham

Lining fabric

Card for template

Sewing thread

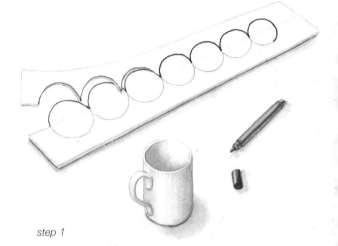

*step 1*

1 Cut a piece of cotton to the length and width required plus 1" (2.5 cm) seam allowance. Cut a rectangular piece of the lining to the same measurements as the cotton. Measure 4¾" (12 cm) in from the outside edges of the lining fabric and cut out, leaving just a rectangular frame. Make a template for the scallops using the card and a round object, such as a cup or small plate, as a guide. Draw a three-quarter circle at one end of the template for the corners of the tablecloth. Trace the outline of the scallops with a marker pen and cut out the card template.

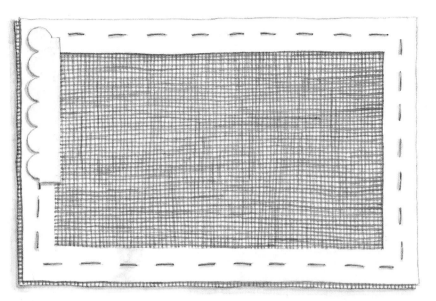

*step 2*

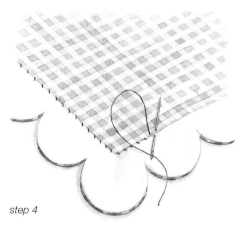

*step 4*

2 With the right sides together, pin and baste the band of lining fabric to the outside edges of the cotton. Using the template and tailor's chalk, trace the outline of the scallops ⅝" (1.5 cm) in from the outside edges.

4 Turn the scallop border right side out and press. Hand stitch the lining to the wrong side of the cotton to hold in place.

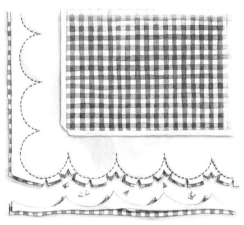

*step 3*

3 Stitch around each scallop along the traced line. Trim back the excess fabric around each scallop to ⅝" (1.5 cm) and make snips every 2" (5 cm) so that the fabric lies flat. Clip the inside corners of the lining fabric to ⅝" (1.5 cm). Remove the basting stitches, fold back and press.

## Materials

Lightweight cotton fabric, such as gingham

Velvet ribbon or rickrack

Sewing thread

*step 1*

**1** Cut a piece of cotton to 20" (50 cm) square. With the fabric right side up, turn in to the front ³⁄₁₆" (0.5 cm) all around, press and baste.

**2** Cut a length of ribbon to 82" (208 cm). Starting at one corner and with outside edges aligning, pin the ribbon to the edge of the hemmed napkin. Miter each corner by making small folds and tucking them under. Cut the two raw ends at 45-degree angles and fold under to form another miter on the final corner. Baste, then machine down both outside edges of the ribbon.

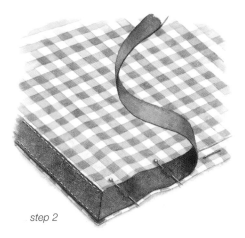

*step 2*

# denim place mats

Add a splash of fun color to your table at the same time as protecting the surface from hot plates or food and beverage stains. Sturdy denim is practical and tightly woven so there is little fraying and it now comes in many colors. Contrasting bias binding and embroidery thread add a little zip to the denim.

# denim place mats

If you can, use a thin padded cotton for the interlining of these place mats so that the bias binding can easily incorporate the layers. For heavier pots and casseroles, use a thicker interlining and a wider bias binding.

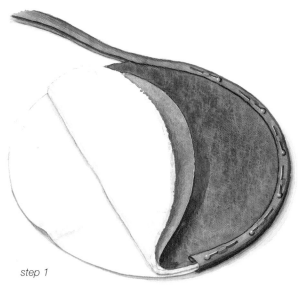

*step 1*

1 Cut circles of the denim, interlining and lining. Baste the three layers together, keeping the interlining in the middle. Pin the bias binding around the circumference, sandwiching the three layers, and baste in place.

2 Using embroidery floss, sew small running stitches around the outside edge to secure the bias binding over the three layers. Again using a running stitch, embroider the place mats in either concentric circles or spirals.

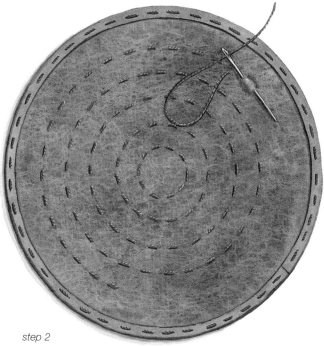

*step 2*

## Materials

Denim

Thin padded cotton
interlining

Lining

Ready-made bias
binding

Sewing thread

Embroidery floss

# monogrammed
# picnic rug

So many wonderful mold- and waterproof fabrics are available nowadays that we no longer need heavy plastic-backed blankets. Make your own personalized picnic rug with a monogram and large rickrack edging to add a little style and amusement to outdoor dining.

# monogrammed picnic rug

Add a monogram to the front of the rug or, if you prefer, a flower or any other favorite motif. I have also made a smaller picnic rug for my dog and added a large bone motif to the center!

1 Cut a piece of both the wool and the backing fabric to the size required plus an extra ¾" (2 cm) seam allowance. Cut a length of the rickrack to the perimeter of the rug. Cut an extra piece of the backing fabric large enough for the monogram.

**Materials**

Wool for front, such as tartan

Waterproof fabric for backing

Paper template for monogram

Embroidery floss

Large rickrack braid

Sewing thread

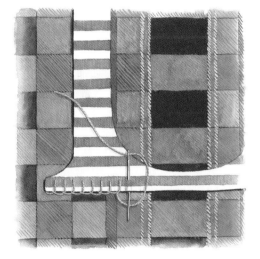

*step 2*

2 Lay the paper template for the monogram over the right side of the small piece of backing fabric, making certain it is on the straight grain, and trace the outline with tailor's chalk. Cut out the monogram. Lay this over the center of the wool tartan, right sides up, pin and baste. Using blanket stitch and embroidery floss, sew the monogram to the front of the wool.

*step 3*

3 With the wool front right side up, lay the rickrack along the outside edge, pin and baste. Stitch along the middle of the rickrack.

*step 4*

4 Lay the piece of backing fabric over the wool front, right side down, and pin. Baste together exactly along the middle of the rickrack (you will have to keep lifting the top layer to guide you). Leave an opening of about 16" (40 cm) along one side. Stitch along basting line. Turn right side out and press. Close the opening using neat slip stitches.

monogrammed picnic rug     135

# fitted tablecloth with box pleats

Disguise an old or unattractive side table with a fitted box-pleated cloth edged in luxurious velvet ribbon. Give the cloth a glamorous look with a fairly long skirt, but don't take it right to the floor — an instant dust collector. The cotton ticking I've used here is durable and washable, as are cotton velvets.

# fitted tablecloth with box pleats

The deep box pleats give this skirt a flounced and fun look. Lining up the stripes requires a little planning, so less-experienced sewers might find it easier to use a narrow stripe or a plain fabric.

1 Cut a piece of the cotton fabric to the size of the tabletop plus an extra ¾" (2 cm) seam allowance all the way around. Cut a strip to measure three times the perimeter of the table by the drop required and add ¾" (2 cm) seam allowance all the way around. (Join pieces for the length if necessary.) Cut a piece of the velvet welting to the perimeter of the table plus an extra ¾" (2 cm). Cut a piece of the velvet ribbon to three times the perimeter of the table plus an extra 1½" (3.75 cm).

*step 2*

2 Lay the cotton for the top panel right side up. Align the raw edges of the velvet welting ¾" (2 cm) from the edges of the panel, making right angles at the corners. Baste in place.

## Materials

Heavy cotton fabric, such as ticking

Velvet welting

Velvet ribbon

Sewing thread

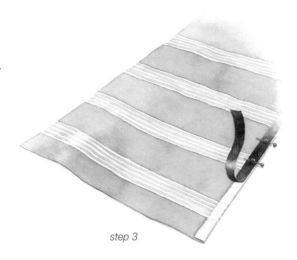

*step 3*

3 Lay the long strip of cotton for the skirt right side up and turn up one long side ³⁄₁₆" (0.5 cm) and press. Lay the velvet ribbon along this fold to cover. Pin, baste and then stitch.

4 Join the two short ends of the skirt ¾" (2 cm) from each edge, open out seam and press flat.

*step 5*

5 Decide on the number of pleats, making sure there are an equal number on opposite sides of

the center panel and one at each corner. Divide the perimeter of the panel by the number of pleats to give the distance between pleats. Pin the top edge to secure each pleat, folding the excess fabric to the back to make the pleat. Check that the skirt fits the center panel. Pin the other end of each pleat and press. Baste along the top edge and machine ¾" (2 cm) from the edge.

*step 6*

6 To assemble the tablecloth, lay the top panel with the velvet welting right side up. With raw edges aligning, place the skirt right side down along the edges of the top panel. Carefully pin the skirt so that the stitched lines are together and the velvet welting is snug between the layers. Baste, then machine stitch using the zipper foot of the machine to sew as closely as possible to the cord. Snip the corners and trim back any excess fabric. To prevent fraying, zigzag the raw edges. Turn right side out and press.

fitted tablecloth with box pleats    139

# organdy tablecloth with napkins

There is something very special and festive about crisp, white linen organdy. Here it is teamed with giant gold polka dots that work equally as well for a traditional holiday lunch as for a special summer wedding party.

# organdy tablecloth with napkins

The polka dots are hand sewn to the organdy cloth and napkins in a random pattern using a lightweight gold thread. For a neat finish, the trick is to get the circles as round as possible when turning under the hem.

2 Using the template and tailor's chalk, trace out as many circles on the gold fabric as you decide to use. Cut out. Pin the circles to the right side of the cloth in a random polka-dot pattern. Turn under the perimeter of each circle as little as possible, press and baste into position.

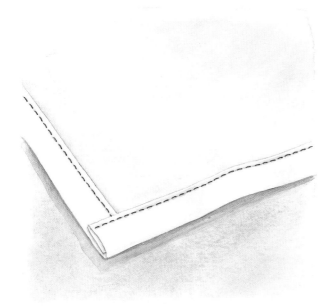

*step 1*

1 Cut the organdy to the size required plus an extra 4" (10 cm) all the way around. Turn under both ends 2" (5 cm) twice, press and baste. Turn in both sides in the same way, keeping the corners neat. Stitch close to the edge of the folds.

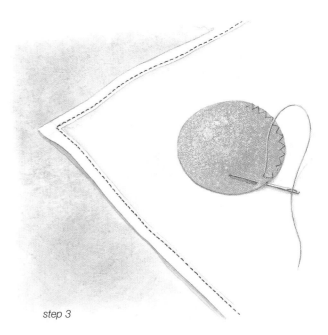

*step 3*

3 Using the gold embroidery floss, hand sew each circle in place with zigzag stitches. Make the napkins in the same way but scale everything down, including the size of the polka dots.

## Materials

Lightweight fine
linen organdy

Sewing thread

Card template of
circle, ³⁄₁₆" (0.5 cm)
larger than required

Gold fabric

Gold embroidery floss

# lampshade skirt with ties

These special decorative skirts sit over paper lampshades to give them an instant new look. Brilliant white organdy works well and would look lovely in a bedroom or dressing room.

# lampshade skirt with ties

**Materials**

Paper for template

Fabric, such as lightweight cotton or organdy

Sewing thread

Instead of organdy, you could use crisp cotton dish towels for a different look. Alternatively, find a lightweight fabric that enhances the colors of your room scheme. Don't use a heavy fabric, as it won't drape or look pert like these skirts do.

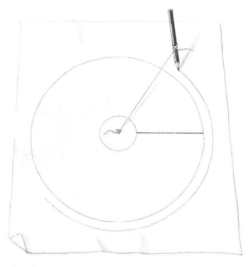

*step 1*

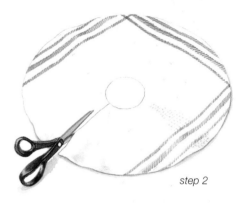

*step 2*

1 Make a paper template of the lampshade that is to be covered. Do this by measuring the diameter of the top and drawing a circle with this diameter plus 2" (5 cm) in the center of the paper. Measure the height of the shade and draw a line from the center circle out by that measurement, adding 1" (2.5 cm). Draw another circle of that diameter. Cut out the card template.

2 Pin the template to a piece of fabric and outline with tailor's chalk. Cut out the fabric, then cut a straight line between the outer and inner circumferences.

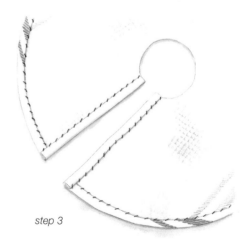

*step 3*

3 Turn under a double ³⁄₁₆" (0.5 cm) hem, press and slip stitch by hand. Do the same along the two straight edges, making neat right-angled folds at the corners.

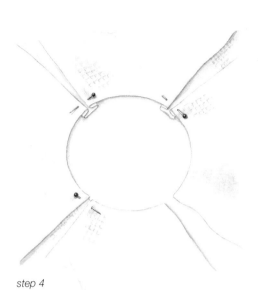

*step 4*

4 Turn the fabric right side up and make three small box pleats around the inner circle, making each inverted pleat about ³⁄₁₆" (0.5 cm). Pin and baste. The inner circle should now have just a slightly larger diameter than the top of the lampshade.

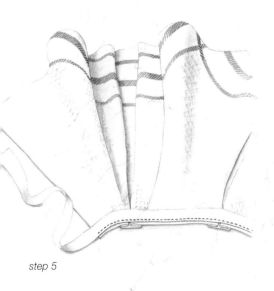

*step 5*

5 Cut a strip of the fabric, on the bias, the diameter of the inner circle plus 18" (46 cm), by ¾" (2 cm). Placing right sides together, center the strip along the top edge of the skirt. Pin and baste ³⁄₁₆" (0.5 cm) below the raw edge. Machine the strip in place ³⁄₁₆" (0.5 cm) from the edge.

6 Turn the strip over the top raw edge of the skirt to hide the machine stitching and fold under ³⁄₁₆" (0.5 cm). Pin and slip stitch by hand. Fold in the raw edges of the tails and slip stitch them together by hand. Press.

# seating

# padded chair cushion

Create a little cushioned comfort for an antique or plain wooden chair. The cushion is shaped to the contours of the chair seat and then attached to the chair back with tailored button-on fabric tabs.

# padded chair cushion

## Materials

Paper for template

Piece of upholstery
foam (1½"/4 cm thick)

Fabric, such as
medium-weight
cotton or linen

Old linen for bottom
of chair cushion

Sewing thread

4 buttons

Use a sturdy fabric for this chair cushion, as it will take a lot of wear and tear.
The antique linen I have used for the bottom of the cushion and the insides of
the tabs adds a smart dressmaker's touch.

**1** Make a template of the chair seat by placing the paper over the seat and tracing its outline, taking care when tracing around the struts. If necessary, tape the paper in place and snip around the struts.

**2** Pin the template to the foam and trace the outline using tailor's chalk. Remove the template and cut out the foam. Lay the same template over a piece of the main fabric and trace the outline using tailor's chalk. Remove the template and cut out, adding a ⅜" (1 cm) seam allowance all the way around. Repeat with the old linen for the bottom of the chair cushion.

**3** For the side panel, cut a strip of the fabric to the length of the perimeter by the thickness of the foam, adding a ⅜" (1 cm) hem allowance all the way around. Join the two short ends with a ⅜" (1 cm) seam, stitch and press the seam open.

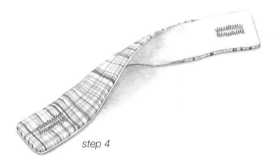

*step 4*

**4** For the ties, cut two strips from both the main fabric and the linen to the length required, adding a ⅜" (1 cm) seam allowance by 1½" (3.75 cm) wide. Lay a strip of the fabric and a strip of the linen right sides together. Pin and baste along both long sides and one short side ⅜" (1 cm) from the edge. Stitch. Turn right side out and press. Fold in the raw edges of the open end. Use small, neat slip stitches to close the opening. Make a buttonhole on both ends of each tie (see page 37).

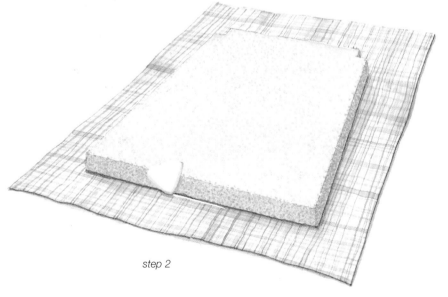

*step 2*

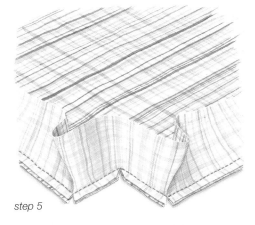

*step 5*

**5** With right sides facing and starting at the center back, pin the side panel to the top panel, taking care to pin it right into the corners. Start stitching 2" (5 cm) from the end of the side panel at the center back, ⅜" (1 cm) from the raw edges. When you get to within 2" (5 cm) of the center back again, adjust the side panel to fit the rest of the back edge and stitch a ⅜" (1 cm) seam in the side panel. Open the seam out and press. Stitch the rest of the side panel to the top panel. Clip the seam allowance around the corners.

**6** Attach the bottom panel to the side panel in the same manner, leaving an opening for the foam. Turn right side out. Press. Sew buttons to the side panel on both sides of two back corners. Insert the foam. Use small, neat slip stitches to close the opening. Button on the ties around the chair struts to secure the cushion in place.

## adding a zipper

To make the cover removable and easier to wash, you could insert a zipper into the bottom of the cushion. Cut two pieces of fabric for the bottom panel and follow the instructions given for inserting a zipper in the Ruffle-edged Pillow on page 18.

# chair cover with ruffle

It's hard to beat the look of a rich, crisp white linen for fresh appeal. Here it is teamed with sharp red-and-white ribbon for a snappy, yet classic, look. A well-fitted chair cover has the same allure as a designer outfit, something special and lasting — yet in this case relatively simple to make. Because it is a slipcover, it can easily be removed for laundering.

# chair cover with ruffle

As your chair is unlikely to be exactly the same shape as the one shown here, you will have to adapt the design to fit. Just remember to make a paper template to ensure a snug fit or, if in doubt, make up a rough sample in cheap muslin or cotton to try out before cutting into an expensive fabric.

**Materials**

Lining fabric for template

Lightweight woven linen

Sewing thread

Striped grosgrain ribbon for edging and ties

**1** Using the lining fabric, make a template of the chair seat, including the top surface and depth of the seat. Mark where the chair struts join the back of the seat.

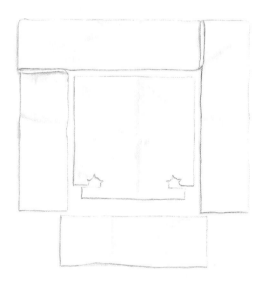

*steps 2 and 3*

**2** Lay the seat template over the linen. Pin, then cut out the center panel, adding ⅜" (1 cm) seam allowance all the way around. Zigzag all raw edges to prevent the linen from fraying. Cut tiny snips around the position of the chair struts, turn in a tiny hem and hand sew to make it neat. Machine darts on the two front corners to fit the seat.

**3** Cut a strip of linen about 8" (20 cm) deep, approximately the length of the front and two sides of the chair seat but adding an extra 12" (30 cm) for gathering. (Join the fabric if necessary.) Cut another strip of linen, again about 8" (20 cm) deep, the length of the back but adding an extra 4" (10 cm) for gathering. Zigzag one long and two short edges of both strips.

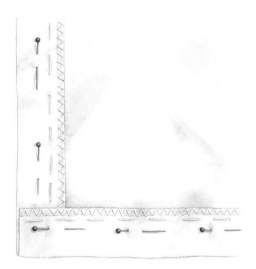

*step 4*

**4** For the front and side skirt, lay the strip of linen right side down. Turn and stitch ⅜" (1 cm) hems along both short sides. Press. Turn and stitch a ⅜" (1 cm) hem along the bottom edge. Press.

*step 5*

5 Cut a piece of ribbon long enough to run along the bottom edge of the front and side skirt, adding an extra ⅜" (1 cm). With the front and side skirt right side up, pin and baste the ribbon to the pressed hem, turning ³⁄₁₆" (0.5 cm) to the back on both side ends. Stitch ribbon in place, taking care to sew only on areas that match the sewing thread. Using strong thread, sew a running stitch along the top edge of the front and side skirt, ⅜" (1 cm) from the edge, leaving long threads at either end. Pull up the threads to make gathers in the skirt to fit the front and sides of the center panel.

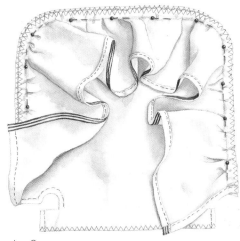

*step 6*

6 Lay the gathered skirt, with right sides together, around the seat top with raw sides edge to edge. Pin and baste the skirt to the seat. Stitch ⅜" (1 cm) from the edge. Repeat steps 4–6 for the back skirt. Turn right side out. Press.

7 Cut four pieces of ribbon for the ties. Hand stitch the ribbon to both sides of the back corners. Tie the ribbons around the struts of the chair to secure the cover.

# chair cover with box pleats

**Materials**

Paper for template

Fabric, such as floral cotton

Lining fabric

Sewing thread

Even though this is the same chair as shown in the previous project, the cover looks quite different with box pleats made up in a pretty pink floral toile de Jouy. You can really transform the look of a chair just by using different fabrics.

1 Make a template of the chair seat by placing the paper over the seat and tracing its outline, taking care when tracing around the struts. If necessary, tape the paper in place and snip around the struts. Pin this template to a piece of the fabric and trace the outline using tailor's chalk. Remove the template and cut out the chair cover seat, adding a ⅜" (1 cm) seam allowance all the way around. Cut a piece of the lining fabric to the same size using the template.

*step 2*

2 Place the fabric and lining right sides together. Pin, baste and stitch with a ⅜" (1 cm) seam allowance but leaving an opening at the front of the seat cover. Turn right side out, slip stitch the opening together and press.

3 For the ties, cut four pieces of the fabric 12" (30 cm) long by 3" (7.5 cm). Fold in half lengthwise with right sides facing and press. Then stitch along the open long side and one short end with a ⅜" (1 cm) seam allowance. Turn right side out using a pencil or knitting needle and press. Use small, neat slip stitches to close the opening.

4 For the front and side skirt, cut a piece of the fabric 10" (25 cm) deep by three times the length of the front and two sides, adding a ⅜" (1 cm) seam allowance all the way around. For the back panel cut a piece of the fabric 10" (25 cm) deep by three times the width of the back, adding a ⅜" (1 cm) seam allowance all the way around.

5 For the front and side skirt, turn in both short ends ⅜" (1 cm) and press. Stitch. Turn up the bottom hem ⅜" (1 cm) and press. Stitch. Repeat this for the back skirt.

step 6

6 To make the inverted box pleats, follow the instructions in step 5 for Fitted Tablecloth with Box Pleats on page 139.

step 7

7 With right sides together, lay the pleated front and side skirt around the chair cover seat with raw sides edge to edge. Pin, baste and stitch with a ⅜" (1 cm) seam allowance. Repeat for the pleated back skirt. Hand sew the ties to the corners.

# tufted bench cushion

A pretty metal bench needs the comfort of a padded seat cushion, and this smart black-and-white checked fabric is most inviting. The welting gives the cushion some rigidity and shape, while the wool tufts add style and formality.

# tufted bench cushion

Once you have mastered the box cushion, you can use the same technique to make window seats, sofa cushions or floor cushions. The secret is in accurate measuring and lining up any pattern, especially at the front edge of the cushion.

1 Cut two pieces of the fabric to the size of the required cushion, adding a 1¼" (3 cm) seam allowance all the way around (¾"/2 cm of this will be taken up by shrinkage when the tufts go in). For the side panel, cut a strip of the fabric to the perimeter of the cushion, adding 1" (2.5 cm) by the width required. (Join pieces if necessary.)

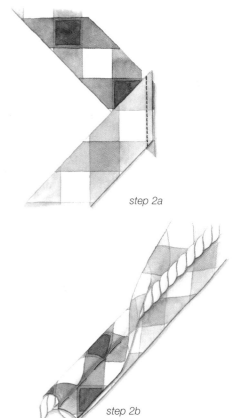

*step 2a*

*step 2b*

2 To make the welting, cut pieces of the fabric on the bias 1½" (4 cm) wide. Join the pieces and press the seam flat. Place the piping cord in the center and wrap the cord in the fabric, wrong sides facing. Baste to enclose the cord without catching it with the stitches. Stitch, using a piping or zipper foot. Make enough welting to go twice around the perimeter of the cushion.

## Materials

Fabric, such as medium-weight cotton or linen

Piping cord

Sewing thread

Batting

Wool or cotton tufts

Flat buttons

*step 3*

3 Pin the welting to the right side of the top panel with the raw sides edge to edge, ⅝" (1.5 cm) from the edge. Baste in place. Pin the side panel over this, right side down, and baste, making sure to avoid sewing into the cord. Machine together as close as possible to the cord.

*step 5*

5 Insert the batting carefully. Hand sew the opening with neat slip stitches to close.

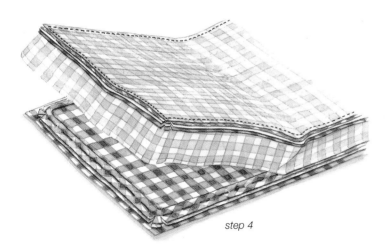

*step 4*

4 Pin another length of the welting to the right side of the bottom panel, with raw sides edge to edge. Baste as close as possible to the cord. Carefully lay the top and side panels over this and baste together close to the edge of the cord, leaving an opening at one end for inserting the batting. Stitch.

*step 6*

6 Mark out the spacings for the tufts with pins. Attach a tuft on the top panel by sewing right through the batting to the back and through a button. Secure the other tufts in the same way. The buttons act as anchors for the tufts and help to create the padded effect.

# tailored dining chair cover

Smarten up an upholstered dining chair with a fitted slipcover. The gently shaped scallops soften the hem as well as adding elegance. Slipcovers are so much more practical on dining chairs, as they can be taken off for laundering in a flash.

# tailored dining chair cover

**Materials**

Fabric

Lining

Paper for template

Sewing thread

The hardest part of this project is achieving a pleasing scalloped pattern to suit the chair. Experiment with paper templates and hold them to the front and sides of the chair to see if your design will work, especially at the corners.

**1** Cut a piece of fabric to the width plus twice the depth of the inside back of the chair, by the height plus the depth of the inside back, adding a ⅝" (1.5 cm) seam allowance all the way around. Cut a piece of fabric the width by the height of the chair outside back, adding a ⅝" (1.5 cm) seam allowance all the way around. For the seat top, cut a piece of fabric the width by the depth of the seat, adding a ⅝" (1.5 cm) seam allowance all the way around. For the skirts, cut four pieces of fabric and of lining to the maximum drop required, by the widths for the front, the back and each side, adding a ⅝" (1.5 cm) seam allowance all around. The width of each side panel must extend to the back edge of the back leg.

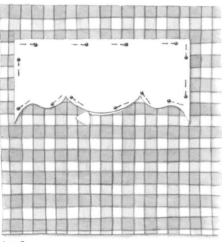

*step 2*

**2** If the sides, front and back of the seat are the same width, make one template by cutting a piece of paper to the width and drop required, and drawing a shallow scallop pattern. Cut out and pin

to wrong side of a side panel. Using tailor's chalk, trace the outline onto the fabric. Cut out, adding a ⅝" (1.5 cm) seam allowance all around. Repeat for the other panels and the lining. (If the sides are different widths, make a template for each one.)

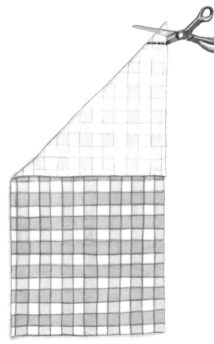

*step 3*

**3** For the inside back panel, take the larger piece of fabric and fold the top with right sides facing to make a 45-degree angle. Mark the depth of the chair back across the top corner and baste a straight line to form a triangle. Stitch and cut away the excess fabric. Repeat for the other side to complete the second fitted dart for the inside back.

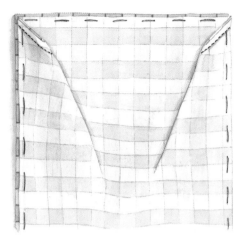

*step 4*

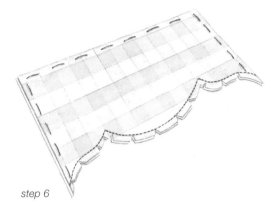

**4** Lay the outside back panel right side up and place the darted inside back panel over the top, right side down, and align all raw edges. Pin and baste ⅝" (1.5 cm) from the raw edges. Stitch the sides and top only, snipping the corners.

**6** For the skirts, take one piece of the fabric and one piece of the lining and lay right sides together. Pin and baste. Machine together along the shaped edge, ³⁄₁₆" (0.5 cm) from the edge. Cut away the excess fabric and snip every 2" (5 cm). Remove the basting. Turn right side out and press. Repeat for all the panels.

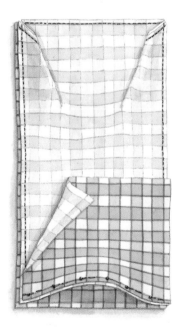

*step 5*

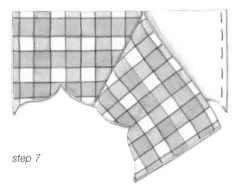

*step 7*

**7** Join the four panels together by laying two panels with right sides facing, pinning and basting ⅝" (1.5 cm) from the short ends. Stitch, open out seams and press. Repeat to join all the panels like a frame.

**5** With right sides together, attach the seat top to the inside back panel, aligning the raw edges. Pin and baste ⅝" (1.5 cm) from the edge. Stitch together.

**8** To attach the skirts to the top, pin right sides together, aligning the raw edges to the front and sides of the seat panel and the bottom edge of the outside back panel, leaving ⅝" (1.5 cm) seam allowances all the way around.

# dining chair cover with ruffle

Although this is the same chair as in the previous project, a very different effect has been achieved by using a floral fabric and richly colored velvet. They combine to make a softly gathered skirt, that gives the chair a romantic and pretty feel.

## Materials

Fabric

Sewing thread

Velvet ribbon

1 Cut a piece of fabric to the width plus twice the depth of the inside back of the chair, by the height plus the depth of the inside back, adding a ⅝" (1.5 cm) seam allowance all the way around. Cut a piece of fabric the width plus 8" (20 cm) for an inverted pleat, by the height of the chair outside back, adding a ⅝" (1.5 cm) seam allowance all the way around. For the seat top, cut a piece of fabric the width and depth of the seat, adding a ⅝" (1.5 cm) seam allowance all the way around. For the gathered skirt, cut a piece of fabric four times the perimeter of the chair seat by the drop required, adding a ⅝" (1.5 cm) seam allowance all the way around. Join pieces where necessary.

2 For the inside back panel, take the larger piece of fabric and, with right sides facing, fold the top to make a 45-degree angle. Mark the depth of the chair back across the top corner and baste a straight line to form a triangle. Stitch and cut away the excess fabric. Repeat for the other side to complete the second fitted dart for the inside back.

*step 2*

*step 3*

3 For the outside back, form the inverted pleat down the center and pin, then baste ⅝" (1.5 cm) from the top edge. With right sides facing, join the inside and outside back by aligning the raw edges, pinning and basting ⅝" (1.5 cm) from edges around both sides and the top only. Machine. Attach the seat top to the inside back panel, right sides together, aligning the raw edges. Pin and baste ⅝" (1.5 cm) from edge. Stitch together.

*step 4*

**4** For the skirt, stitch the two short ends together. Open out the seam and press. Turn up the bottom hem, right sides facing, to just less than the width of the ribbon, pin and baste. Cut a length of the velvet ribbon to the perimeter of the skirt. Pin, then baste it over the hem and machine along both outer edges to secure the ribbon.

*step 5*

**5** Sew two parallel rows of running stitch ⅜" (1 cm) from the top edge of the skirt and gather it up evenly to measure the same as the perimeter of the seat top (including the opened out pleat). With the right sides facing, align the raw edges of the skirt with the seat top and the bottom edge of the outside back. Pin and baste together. Machine ⅝" (1.5 cm) from the edge. Turn right side out and press. Cut three pairs of velvet ties and hand sew them to the back to close the pleat.

# beaded armchair cover

Give a family heirloom a new lease on life with a gorgeous linen fitted slipcover trimmed with perky ceramic beads. On an old armchair, the fit doesn't need to be perfect. In fact, the odd gather and tuck add a casual elegance reminiscent of comfortable old country houses.

# beaded armchair cover

**Materials**

Fabric

Sewing thread

Heavy beading on
tape

This technique takes time, but it's more than worth it when you have a smart
new cover for an old chair. Leave plenty of extra fabric in the seam allowances
for adjusting the fabric to fit.

*steps 1 and 2*

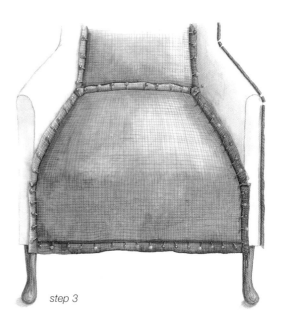

*step 3*

2 Cut a length of fabric for one of the outside side
panels, adding 3" (7.5 cm) all the way around
for seams. Pin to the side, wrong side out. When
cutting around a shaped area, make small snips in
the fabric every 1" (2.5 cm) to help the fabric ease
around the curves. Repeat for the other side.

1 Cut a length of the fabric for the inside back of
the chair, adding a 3" (7.5 cm) seam allowance
all the way around. Using dressmaker's pins, pin the
panel, wrong side out, to the inside back of the chair.

3 Cut a piece of fabric for the seat, including
the drop at the front of the chair, adding
3" (7.5 cm) all the way around for seams. Pin to
the chair with the fabric wrong side out.

*step 4*

4 Cut a piece of fabric for one of the inside side panels, adding 3" (7.5 cm) all around for seams. Pin to the chair with the wrong side out. Repeat for the other side.

*step 5*

5 Cut a strip of the fabric for the front of the arms, taking it from the top right down to bring it level with the bottom edge of the seat. With the wrong side out, pin this to the chair and repeat for the other arm.

6 For the outside back, cut a length of the fabric, adding 3" (7.5 cm) all the way around for the seams. If the back on your chair splays out at the top, cut the panel to the wider measurement all the way down to allow the cover to be pulled over the chair. Pin the panel to the back, wrong side out.

*step 6*

7 Trim off all excess fabric to leave a ¾" (2 cm) seam allowance. Remove the pins one by one and replace them with dressmaker's pins and then pin the fabric pieces together, making smooth seam lines. Once you have gone over the whole chair, carefully gather up the cover. Baste along the pinned edges. Remove the pins and stitch. Turn up the hem to the drop required, pin and baste. Pin the beading to the outside edge of the hem and stitch to incorporate the hem. Press.

# simple sofa cover

A crisp, cotton slipcover in a romantic floral print brings instant summer breeziness to any sofa — an effective transformation for any worn piece of old furniture. Once you have mastered the technique, you'll be hooked!

# simple sofa cover

If this is your first attempt at a slipcover, it is probably best to start with a small and clean-lined sofa with few cushions. Although it is a logical process, the fewer panels you have to join together, the easier the project.

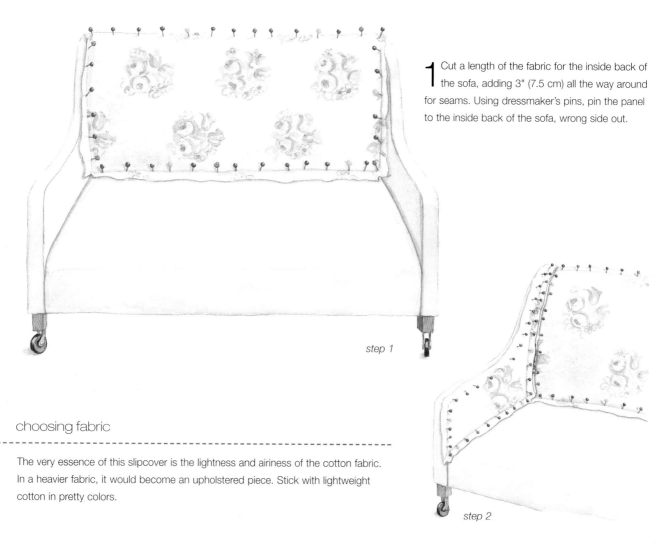

1 Cut a length of the fabric for the inside back of the sofa, adding 3" (7.5 cm) all the way around for seams. Using dressmaker's pins, pin the panel to the inside back of the sofa, wrong side out.

*step 1*

*step 2*

## choosing fabric

The very essence of this slipcover is the lightness and airiness of the cotton fabric. In a heavier fabric, it would become an upholstered piece. Stick with lightweight cotton in pretty colors.

2 Cut fabric for one of the inside arm panels, adding 3" (7.5 cm) all around for seams. Pin to the sofa, wrong side out. Repeat for the other side.

## Materials

Fabric

Sewing thread

*step 3*

**3** Cut a length of the fabric for the seat, including the drop at the front, and adding 3" (7.5 cm) all around for seams. Pin to the sofa, wrong side out.

*step 4*

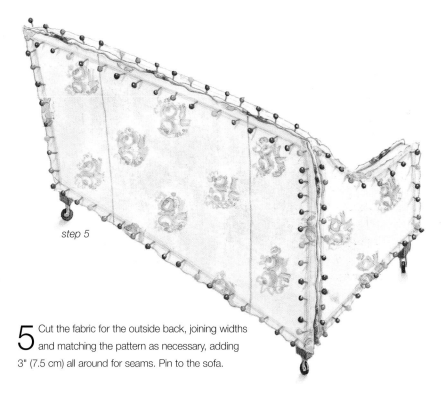

*step 5*

**4** Cut a piece of fabric for one of the outside arm panels, adding 3" (7.5 cm) all around for seams. Pin to the sofa, wrong side out.

**5** Cut the fabric for the outside back, joining widths and matching the pattern as necessary, adding 3" (7.5 cm) all around for seams. Pin to the sofa.

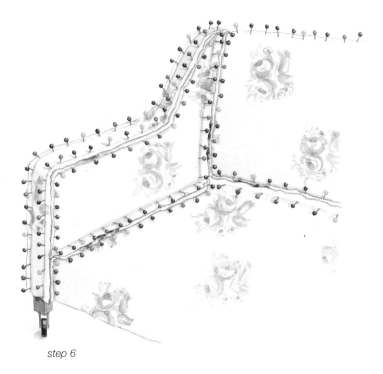

*step 6*

*step 9*

**8** For each seat cushion, cut out two pieces of fabric the size of the seat cushion, adding ¾" (2 cm) all the way around for seams. Cut a side panel from the fabric to the same length as the perimeter by the width of the cushion, adding ¾" (2 cm) all the way around for seams.

**6** Cut a piece of fabric for panel along the top of each sofa arm, adding 3" (7.5 cm) all around for seams. Pin to the arms, wrong side out.

**7** Trim off all excess fabric to leave a ¾" (2 cm) seam allowance all the way around. Remove the pins one by one and repin the fabric pieces together, making smooth seam lines. Once you have gone over the whole sofa, carefully take the cover off. Baste along the pinned edges. Remove the pins and machine. Turn up the hem to the drop required, pin and baste. Stitch.

**9** With the right sides facing, pin, then baste the side to the top panel. Stitch ¾" (2 cm) from the edges, snipping the corners.

**10** Attach the bottom panel with the right sides facing, leaving an opening at the back for inserting the cushion form. Turn right side out. Insert the cushion form and hand sew the opening with small, neat hand stitches to close.

## allowing for shrinkage

Slipcovers inevitably take some wear and tear, so they need to be laundered. Make sure the slipcover is large enough to allow for any shrinkage. If necessary, wash a small sample of the fabric to check for shrinkage.

# beanbag with handles

You will have the whole family competing for this huge squashy beanbag — even the pets! Made in chic linen toile de Jouy and finished with velvet welting, it's the perfect place to relax. Big handles make it easy to move the beanbag around the house.

# beanbag with handles

It's tempting to overfill a beanbag with beads, but this makes it uncomfortable to sit in. You will need to experiment before sewing it up, but remember that the beads will compact a bit with time.

1 Cut two circles of the fabric to the desired size, adding an extra ⅝" (1.5 cm) seam allowance all the way around. Measure the circumference of the circle and divide this by four. Then cut four panels of fabric for the sides to this measurement by the height required, adding a ⅝" (1.5 cm) seam allowance all the way around.

*step 2*

2 Lay one of the side panels right side up. Cut a length of the velvet welting to the height of the panel and lay over one end, aligning the raw edges. Pin, then baste into place. Using a piping or zipper foot, machine close to the cord. Then lay another panel over the top of this, right side down, and pin close to the cord, then baste. Machine down. Join all four panels in this way.

## Materials

Fabric

Velvet welting

Sewing thread

Sack of beads for filling

*step 3*

**3** For each handle, cut two strips of fabric 12" (30 cm) by 4" (10 cm). Fold in half lengthwise, right sides facing. Press. Machine the long sides and one short side. Turn right side out, press and close the end with small, neat slip stitches. Machine the ends of each handle to the right side of opposite panels.

*step 4*

**4** Lay the top panel right side up and cut a piece of the velvet welting to the circumference of the circle. With raw edges aligning, pin, then baste the piping to the outside edge, tapering the ends off into the seam allowance. Repeat for the bottom panel.

**5** Lay the top panel right side up and carefully put the side panels over the top, right side down, aligning the raw edges. Pin and baste. Machine, taking care to stitch close to the velvet welting and through all the layers.

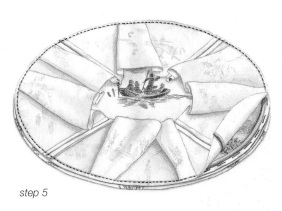

*step 5*

**6** To attach the bottom panel, lay it right side up and carefully align the remaining raw edges of the side panels, right sides down, around the perimeter. Pin, baste and then machine together, leaving a gap for inserting the filling. Turn right side out. Fill with beads and close up using small, neat slip stitches.

# sources

To follow is a selection of manufacturers and retailers of fabrics, wallcoverings, trim and window hardware in North America. Please remember that the toll-free numbers usually work in the originating country only.

**ABC Carpet and Home**
888 Broadway
New York, NY 10003
Tel: (212) 473-3000
www.abchome.com
*Fabrics including silks, velvets and taffetas*

**Arlene's Interiors**
751 Terminal Avenue
Vancouver, BC V6A 2M2
Toll-free: (888) 275-3637
Tel: (604) 608-1177
www.arlenes.com
*Fabrics including chenilles, velvets and cottons*

**Belmont Home Decor**
4201 West Belmont Avenue
Chicago, IL 60641
Toll-free: (800) 282-1671
www.belmonthomedecor.com
*Online purchasing available*
*Fabrics and trim*

**Bergamo Fabrics**
P.O. Box 231
Mount Vernon, NY 10551-0231
Tel: (914) 665-0800
www.bergamofabrics.com
*Showrooms across the U.S.*
*Fabrics including silks, cottons and linens*

**Brewster Wallcovering Company**
Toll-free: (800) 366-1700
www.brewp.com
*In stores across the U.S.*
*Fabrics and wallcoverings*

**Brunschwig & Fils**
www.brunschwig.com
*In stores across the U.S.*
*Fabrics and trim*

**Calico Corners**
Toll-free: (800) 213-6366
www.calicocorners.com
*In stores across the U.S.*
*Phone and mail order purchasing available*
*Fabrics and trim*

**The Carol Harris Company**
1265 South Main
Dyersburg, TN 38024
Tel: (713) 285-9419
www.carolharrisco.com
*Online and mail order purchasing available*
*Fabrics, lace, trim and sewing accessories*

**Chintz & Company**
Stores in Vancouver, BC;
Victoria, BC; Edmonton, AB;
Calgary, AB
www.chintz.com
*Fabrics, tassels, trim and window hardware*

**Denver Fabrics**
2777 West Belleview
Denver, CO 80123-2953
Toll-free: (866) 996-4573
Tel: (303) 730-2777
www.denverfabrics.com
*Online purchasing available*
*Fabric and sewing accessories*

**Designer Fabrics International**
1360 Queen Street West
Toronto, ON M6K 1L7
Tel: (416) 531-2810
www.designerfabrics.ca
*Online and phone purchasing available*
*Discount high-end fabrics and trim*

**Donghia**
485 Broadway
New York, NY 10013
Tel: (212) 925-2777
www.donghia.com
*In showrooms across the U.S.*
*Fabrics and trim*

**Fabric.com**
Toll-free: (888) 455-2940
www.fabric.com
*Online purchasing only*
*Fabrics and sewing accessories*

**Fabricadabra**
Toll-free: (800) 820-9328
Tel: (508) 497-9300
www.fabricadabra.us
*Online purchasing only*
*Fabrics*

**Fabricland**
www.fabricland.ca
*170 stores across Canada*
*Fabrics, accessories and sewing supplies*

**Great Windows**
12011 Guilford Road
Suite 104A
Annapolis Junction, MD
20701
Toll-free: (800) 556-6632
www.greatwindows.com
*Online and mail order*
*purchsing available*
*Fabrics and window*
*hardware*

**Hancock Fabrics**
3406 West Main Street
Tupelo, MS 38801
Toll-free: (877) 322-7427
www.hancockfabrics.com
*In stores across the U.S.*
*Online, phone and mail order*
*purchasing available*
*Fabrics, accessories and*
*sewing supplies*

**Harlequin**
5100 Highlands Parkway
Smyrna, GA 30082
Tel: (678) 303-9999
and
Beauport Wallcoverings
1400 Graham Bell
Boucherville, QC J4B 6E5
Tel: (450) 641-4477
www.harlequin.uk.com
*Distributed worldwide*
*Contemporary fabrics and*
*wallcoverings*

**Interior Mall**
Toll-free: (800) 590-5844
Tel: (497) 492-3025
www.interiormall.com
*Online and phone purchasing*
*only*
*Fabrics and accessories*

**Jo-Ann Fabrics**
Toll-free: (888) 739-4120
www.joann.com
*In stores across the U.S.*
*Online purchasing available*
*Fabrics and sewing*
*accessories*

**L.P. Thur Inc.**
126 West 23rd Street
New York, NY 10011
Toll-free: (800) 582-2624
Tel: (212) 243-4702
www.fabricoutlet.com
*Online purchasing available*
*Fabrics*

**Lee Joffa**
Toll-free U.S.: (800) 453-3563
Toll-free Canada: (888) 533-5632
www.leejofa.com
*In showrooms across the*
*U.S. and Canada*
*Fabrics and trim*

**Lulu DK Fabrics**
Tel: (212) 223-4234
www.luludk.com
*In stores across the U.S.*
*Fabrics and wallcoverings*

**Pierre Deux**
Toll-free: (888)743-7732
www.pierredeux.com
*In stores across the U.S.*
*Fabrics*

**Pierre Frey**
Pierre Frey Inc.
15 East 32nd Street 6th Floor
New York, NY 10016
Tel: (212) 213-3099
www.pierrefrey.com
*Fabrics and trim*

**Restoration Hardware**
Toll-free: (800) 762-1005
www.restorationhardware.com
*Stores located across North*
*America*
*Online, phone and mail order*
*purchasing available*
*Window hardware and*
*drapery rods*

**Sahco Hesslein**
www.sahco-hesslein.com
*In showrooms across the*
*U.S. and in Montreal*
*Fabrics including modern*
*viscose, linens and silks*

**Sanderson**
www.sanderson-uk.com
*Distributed throughout North*
*America*
*Fabrics and accessories*

**Sawyer Brook Distinctive**
**Fabrics**
P.O. Box 1800W
Clinton, MA 01510-0813
Toll-free: (800) 290-2739
Tel: (978) 368-3133
www.sawyerbrook.com
*Online and mail order*
*purchasing available*
*Fabrics and sewing*
*accessories*

**Scalamdre**
www.scalamandre.com
*Showrooms across North*
*America*
*Fabrics and trim*

**Waverly**
Toll-free: (800) 988-7775
www.waverly.com
*In stores throughout North*
*America*
*Online and phone purchasing*
*of fabric samples available*
*Fabric and trim*

# index

**A**

appliqué-decorated pillow 39, 42, 43

armchair covers

  beaded 170-73

  *see also* sofa cover, simple

**B**

beaded armchair cover 170-73

bean bag with handles 180-83

bed linen, tailored

  dust ruffle 118-19

  quilt cover and pillowcases 114-17

bedspreads

  cotton-backed wool bedspread 96-99

  fleece throw with pompoms 100-101

  lace-edged coverlet 90-93

  patchwork throw 106-109

  ribbon-decorated coverlet 94-95

  ruffle-edged eiderdown 102-105

bench cushions

  tufted 160-63

  *see also* box floor cushion

blanket stitch 100

bolsters

  with gingham rose 25

  with silk ties 22-24

box floor cushion 30-33

box-pleated chair cover 158-59

box-pleated tablecloth 136-39

buttoned pillow sleeve 34-37

**C**

chair covers

  beaded (for armchairs) 170-73

  with box pleats 158-59

  with ruffle 154-57

  with ruffle (for dining chairs) 168-69

  tailored (for dining chairs) 164-67

*see also* sofa cover, simple

clip-on drapes 46-49

contrast lined drapes 50-53

cot quilt with embroidered initial 110-13

cotton-backed wool bedspread 96-99

coverlets

  lace-edged 90-93

  ribbon-decorated 94-95

cushion, padded (for wooden chairs) 150-53

**D**

denim place mats 128-31

dining chair covers

  with ruffle 168-69

  tailored 164-67

dog beds *see* bean bag with handles; box floor cushion

drapes

  basic clip-on 46-49

  contrast lined 50-53

  edgings for 67

  lined, with tiebacks 60-63

  ruffle-edged 64-67

  semi-sheer panels 68-71

  swag 72-75

  unlined, with sewn ties 58-59

  unlined, with tape ties 54-57

**E**

edgings, curtain 67

eiderdown, ruffle-edged 102-105

embroidered initials 112-13

  *see also* monograms

**F**

fabrics

  choosing 9, 93

matching patterns 87

  for patchwork 109

fleece throw with pompoms 100-101

floor cushion, box 30-33

fringing, drape 67

**G**

gathered round pillow 26-29

gingham dust ruffle 118-19

gingham scallop-edged tablecloth and napkins 122-27

**H**

herringbone stitch 113

**I**

initials, embroidered 112-13

  *see also* monograms

**L**

lace-edged coverlet 90-93

lampshade skirt with ties 144-47

laser-cut cotton 53

lined drapes with tiebacks 60-63

lined Roman shade 80-83

loose covers

  for armchairs 170-73

  for dining chairs 164-69

  for sofas 174-79

**M**

mats, table 128-31

monograms

  on shades 76, 83

  on pillow covers 12, 13

  on picnic rug 132-35

  *see also* cot quilt with embroidered initial

**N**

napkins
  gingham 122, 127
  organdie 142-43

**O**

organdie
  lampshade skirt with ties 144-47
  tablecloth with napkins 140-43

**P**

patchwork throw 106-109
picnic rug, monogrammed 132-35
pillowcases, rickrack-trimmed 117
pillow covers
  appliqué-decorated 39, 42, 43
  basic 12
  box floor 30-33
  buttoned sleeve 34-37
  gathered round 26-29
  monogrammed 12, 13
  ribbon-decorated 39, 40-41
  ruffle-edged 16-19
  scallop-edged 20-21
  trimming with piping 15
  trimming with rickrack 15
  tufted bench 160-63
  zipped 18
  see also bolster with silk ties
piping, applying 15, 32, 162-63
place mats, denim 128-31
pleats, drape 63
pompoms, making 100
portière rods 69, 71

**Q**

quilt, cot 110-113
quilt cover and pillowcases, tailored 114-17

**R**

ribbon-decorated coverlet 94-95
ribbon-decorated pillow cover 39, 40-41
rickrack, applying 15, 114, 117
Roman shades
  lined 80-83
  unlined 76-79
rope borders, applying 15
rosettes, fabric 25, 29
ruffle-edged drapes 64-67
ruffle-edged pillow cover 16-19
ruffle-edged eiderdown 102-105
ruffled chair cover 154-57
ruffled dining chair cover 168-69
rug, picnic: with monogram 132-35

**S**

scallop-edged pillow 20-21
scallop-edged tablecloth 122-26
scalloped dining chair covers 164-67
scrim ruffles 66-67
seating
  bean bag with handles 180-83
  box floor cushion 30-33
  padded cushion (for wooden chair) 150-53
  tufted bench cushion 160-63
  see also chair covers; sofa cover, simple
shades
  hiding fixings with swags 72-75
  lined Roman 80-83
  monogrammed 76, 83
  stringing 79
  Swedish roll-up 84-87
  unlined Roman 76-79
sofa cover, simple 174-79
stitches
  blanket 100
  herringbone 113

swags, simple 72-75
Swedish roll-up shade 84-87

**T**

tablecloths
  fitted, with box pleats 136-39
  organdie 140-43
  scallop-edged 122-26
throws
  fleece, with pompoms 100-101
  patchwork 106-109
tiebacks, drape 60-63
ties
  for bolsters 24, 25
  for drapes 54-57 (tape), 58-59 (sewn),
    see also tiebacks, drape
  for pillow covers 40-41
trimmings, applying
  to pillows 15
  to drapes 67
tufted bench cushion 160-63

**U**

unlined drapes with sewn ties 58-59
unlined drapes with tape ties 54-57
unlined Roman shade 76-79

**V**

valance, tailored 118-19

**W**

window seat cushions
  tufted 160-63
  see also box floor cushion

**Z**

zippers: inserting in cushions 18, 153

# photography credits

The following companies supplied fabrics, trimmings, and poles for the projects in this book.

**page 12  simple pillow**
cushion fabric from Brunschwig & Fils

**page 14  trimmed pillows**
top cushion fabric from Brunschwig & Fils, middle cushion fabric from Jane Churchill, antique trimming from Pavilion Antiques, bottom cushion gingham from Jane Churchill, antique blue linen from Pavilion Antiques, rickrack from V.V. Rouleaux

**pages 16-21  ruffle-edged pillow and scallop-edged pillow**
tickings from Ian Mankin

**pages 22-25  bolster with silk ties**
Toile de Jouy and silk from Brunschwig & Fils, rosettes and velvet ribbon from V.V. Rouleaux

**page 26  gathered round pillow**
fabric from Sahco Hesslein

**pages 30-33  box floor cushion**
stripe from Lee Jofa, antique cloth from Tobias & the Angel

**pages 34-37  buttoned pillow sleeve**
Toile de Jouy from Turnell & Gigon, linen from GP&J Baker

**pages 38-43  decorated pillows**
Fabric from Lee Jofa, trimming from V.V. Rouleaux, felt from B. Brown

**pages 46-49  basic clip-on drapes**
felt from B. Brown, clips from Walcot House

**pages 50-53  contrast lined drapes**
Cutwork fabric from Clarence House, silk from Brunschwig & Fils

**pages 54-57  unlined drapes with tape ties**
blue fabric from Monkwell, tape from McCulloch & Wallis

**page 58  unlined drapes with sewn ties**
fabric from Turnell & Gigon

**page 60  lined drapes with tiebacks**
cream linen from GP&J Baker, pink check from Jane Churchill

**pages 64-67  ruffle-edged drapes**
wool from GP&J Baker, scrim from The Natural Fabric Company, edging from Chelsea Textiles

**pages 68–71  semi-sheer curtain panels**
sheer from Zoffany, opaque fabric from GP&J Baker, portière kit from Cameron Fuller

**pages 72-75  simple swag**
yellow linen from Designers Guild, ribbon from V.V. Rouleaux

**pages 76-79  unlined roman shade**
linen from The Cloth Shop, monogramming by Kerry Jupp

**pages 80-83  lined roman shade**
stripe from Morrocan market, gingham from Fabrics Galore, monogram from Guinevere Antiques

**pages 84-87  swedish roll-up shade**
floral fabric from Colefax & Fowler, gingham from Zoffany, glass rings from The Blue Door

**pages 90-92  lace-edged coverlet**
fabric from Lewis & Wood, velvet ribbon from V.V. Rouleaux, antique lace from Tobias & the Angel

**page 95  ribbon-decorated coverlet**
fabric from Lewis & Wood, ribbons from V.V. Rouleaux

**pages 96-98  cotton-backed wool bedspread**

wool fabric from Abbott & Boyd, floral linen from Cath Kidston

**pages 100-101  fleece throw with pompoms**

striped wool blanket from Shaker, cream fleece from Fabrics Galore, pompoms made from Rowan Yarn, embroidered pillowcase from The Volga Linen Co.

**pages 102-104  ruffle-edged eiderdown**

eiderdown made by Eiderdown Studios, floral chintz from Jean Munro, linen gingham from Gingham Goods

**pages 106-109  patchwork throw**

embroidered bedlinen from Shaker

**pages 114-117  tailored bed linen**

ivory linen from Nya Nordiska, rickrack from V.V. Rouleaux

**page 118  tailored dust ruffle**

checked fabric from Manuel Canovas

**pages 122-27  scallop-edged tablecloth and napkins**

gingham scalloped cloth and velvet edged napkins from Gingham Goods

**pages 128-31  denim place mats**

denim from Denim in Style

**page 132-34  monogrammed picnic rug**

tartan from Cabbages & Roses, Sumbrella red stripe from Scalamandre, giant rickrack from V.V. Rouleaux

**pages 136-38  fitted tablecloth with box pleats**

grey ticking from Ian Mankin, velvet ribbon from V.V. Rouleaux

**pages 140-43  organdie tablecloth with napkins**

white organdie from MacCulloch & Wallis, polka dot cookies made by Peggy Porschen Cakes

**pages 150-53  padded chair cushion**

blue fabric from Brunschwig & Fils

**pages 158-59  chair cover with box pleats**

fabric from Jane Churchill

**pages 160-62  tufted bench cushion**

fabric from Pierre Frey

**page 165  tailored dining chair cover**

fabric from Nobilis Fontan

**page 169  dining chair cover with ruffle**

fabric from Abbott & Boyd, velvet ribbon from V.V. Rouleaux, rug from The Rug Company

**page 170  beaded armchair cover**

fabric from Cole & Son, glass beading from V.V. Rouleaux

**pages 175-78  simple sofa cover**

fabric from Cabbages & Roses

**page 181-82  beanbag with handles**

fabric from Zoffany, velvet piping from V.V. Rouleaux

# author's acknowledgments

It takes a real team to produce a book like this, and I had a great one!

My sincerest thanks go to David Montgomery, who took all the photographs for the book, with tireless enthusiasm, in wintry conditions, and with little time—they are wonderful!

Melanie Williams made almost every single item for the book—she worked extraordinarily hard and her sewing is sublime. Thank you.

The artworks are exquisitely painted by Carolyn Jenkins.

Helen Lewis's art direction and quick-witted help on the photo shoots speaks for itself.

Lisa Pendreigh has been a stalwart editor; her attention to detail being of paramount importance for a sewing book.

Thank you to Jane O'Shea and Alison Cathie for asking me to do the book!